INTERRUPTING THE LEGAL PERSON

STUDIES IN LAW, POLITICS, AND SOCIETY

Recent volumes:

Volumes 1–2:	Edited by Rita J. Simon
Volume 3:	Edited by Steven Spitzer
Volumes 4–9:	Edited by Steven Spitzer and Andrew S. Scull
Volumes 10–16:	Edited by Susan S. Sibey and Austin Sarat
Volumes 17–33:	Edited by Austin Sarat and Patricia Ewick
Volumes 34–77:	Edited by Austin Sarat
Volume 78:	Edited by Livia Holden and Austin Sarat
Volume 79:	Edited by Austin Sarat
Volume 80:	Edited by Austin Sarat
Volume 81:	Edited by Austin Sarat
Volume 82:	Edited by Austin Sarat
Volume 83:	Edited by Austin Sarat
Volume 84:	Edited by Austin Sarat
Volume 85:	Edited by Austin Sarat
Volume 86:	Part A: Edited by Austin Sarat
Volume 86:	Part B: Edited by Austin Sarat

STUDIES IN LAW, POLITICS, AND SOCIETY VOLUME 87A

INTERRUPTING THE LEGAL PERSON

EDITED BY

AUSTIN SARAT
Amherst College, USA

GUEST EDITED BY

GEORGE PAVLICH AND RICHARD MAILEY
University of Alberta, Canada

emerald PUBLISHING

United Kingdom – North America – Japan
India – Malaysia – China

Emerald Publishing Limited
Howard House, Wagon Lane, Bingley BD16 1WA, UK

First edition 2022

British Library Cataloguing in Publication Data
A catalogue record for this book is available from the British Library

ISBN: 978-1-80262-864-7 (Print)
ISBN: 978-1-80262-863-0 (Online)
ISBN: 978-1-80262-865-4 (Epub)

ISSN: 1059-4337 (Series)

Printed and bound by CPI Group (UK) Ltd, Croydon, CR0 4YY

ISOQAR certified Management System, awarded to Emerald for adherence to Environmental standard ISO 14001:2004.

ISOQAR REGISTERED
Certificate Number 1985
ISO 14001

INVESTOR IN PEOPLE

CONTENTS

LIST OF CONTRIBUTORS

Jennifer L. Culbert	Johns Hopkins University, USA
Richard Mailey	University of Alberta, Canada
James R. Martel	San Francisco State University, USA
Val Napoleon	University of Victoria, Canada
Shoshana Paget	Concordia University, Canada
George Pavlich	University of Alberta, Canada
Amy Swiffen	Concordia University, Canada
Johan van der Walt	University of Luxembourg, Luxembourg

EDITORIAL BOARD

CHAPTER 1

REFRAMING COLONIAL LAW'S CRIMINALLY ACCUSED PERSONS

George Pavlich

ABSTRACT

This chapter studies a political rationale by which colonial law forged socially assigned individuals as criminally accused persons. Focussing on archived documents of a preliminary examination that took place in 1883 in the North West Territories (now Alberta), it highlights how an accused person was moulded as a culpable individual. Arranged by a justice of the peace, and member of the North West Mounted Police, the investigation in this case reveals how colonial law unleashed an individualising force that obscured power relations behind the settlement it aimed to further. The unequal ways in which certain distinctions of person were legally recognised and individualised may be traced to long-standing western uses of social hierarchies as 'masks' from which law unequally recognised persons. Challenging such approaches to personhood, the analysis works off Naffine's 'legalistic' ideas of persons as fictions, calling for a retelling of the fictions around accused persons. By pointing out the possibility of accusing relational rather than individual constructions, it concludes with a brief insinuation of legal forms directed at 'collective persons', interrupting a key political logic of colonial criminal law with allied promises of social justice beyond colonisation.

Keywords: Criminal accusation; legal persons; colonial criminalisation; settler-Colonial Law; postcolonial justice; indigenous law

Interrupting the Legal Person
Studies in Law, Politics, and Society, Volume 87A, 1–17

Published under exclusive licence by Emerald Publishing Limited
ISSN: 1059-4337/doi:10.1108/S1059-43372022000087A001

INTRODUCTION

The disproportionate numbers of Indigenous people in Canada's criminal justice institutions, signalling an enduring colonial legacy, has been well documented (e.g., Cunneen & Tauri, 2016; Monchalin, 2016). What is less well known is how such an inequality might be related to a persistent political logic at opening socio-cultural instants of criminalisation, at moments where selected persons are hailed into being as criminally accused individuals. Forming these subjects echoes an ancient Greek use of the word 'accuse', which was related to *kategoria* and debates over how best to categorise happenings (Antaki, 2017); but it also connotes the Latin *crimen* that suggests (among other senses) a 'calling to account' (Ayto, 2011). The importance of accusatory openings to colonial law's ways of calling subjects to account is nicely captured in a courtroom drama described in J. M. Coetzee's *Schooldays of Jesus*. Readers encounter an accused individual standing before a court, blithely declaring his acceptance of its accusations and charges of guilt. The judge responds with a vigorous reproach:

> You say further that you do not want to save yourself. But your salvation is not a matter that rests in your hands. If we, your judges, do not do our best to save you, following scrupulously the letter of the law, then we will have failed to save the law … we have a responsibility to society, a grave and onerous responsibility …. But we have an equal responsibly to save you the accused from yourself, in the event that you are or were not yourself as the law understands being oneself to be. Am I clear? (Coetzee, 2016, Kindle Loc 2063–2068)

Thus, law is 'saved' so long as it maintains concepts of the persons it accuses and targets, and upon which its gaze alights. Forging such persons is a foundational – if fictional – matter for law, and one that starts with procedures that mould accused persons to face particular kinds of legal scrutiny. This is why Agamben insists that, 'what defines the trial is neither guilt (which is unnecessary in archaic law) nor punishment but rather the accusation'; that is, 'the accusation is perhaps the juridical "category" par excellence (*kategoria* means "accusation" in Greek), without which the whole edifice of law would fall apart' (Agamben, 2011, p. 23). Hence, from this vantage, criminal law is founded on the accusations that categorise and shape 'persons' who are called to account in law, with implications for the criminal justice institutions that such processes unevenly populate.

With this approach in mind, the following chapter discusses an 1883 case in which a 'preliminary examination' in the Dominion of Canada's North West Territories (NWT) is highlighted, focussing on a governmental logic that targeted individual persons at accusatory thresholds to a colonial criminal law. Although this law's local deployment was explicitly designed to foster Dominion capitalist settlement, the idea of 'settler colonialism' (Veracini, 2014) was here still very much in process – following the arrival of the North West Mounted Police (NWMP), and the making of Treaties 6 (in 1876) and 7 (in 1877). Even so, emerging prejudices, identities, and divisions congruent with contested migrations from Eastern Canada, Europe, etc., are reflected by attempts to unleash Dominion criminal law to secure its visions of a settled order (Nettelbeck, Smandych, Knafla, & Foster, 2016). Further, the selected case exemplifies local practices of criminalisation in the making, reminding us that the NWT relied on preliminary examinations rather than grand juries to fix accused bodies as individuals who could confront an unfolding criminal law. Specifically, at thresholds to criminalisation, as arranged by commissioned justices of the peace, preliminary examinations materialised around a politics of masking that first imputed group membership to avowers and then relied on 'individual' testimony when judging whether to send an accused to trial. Colonial criminalisation was thus initiated by recognising specific kinds of persons in society before focussing that gaze on the *individual* persons it cast as the accused.

Although these notions of legal persons have immediate roots in imperialising English common law, their colonial appearance simultaneously traced western discursive genealogies of personhood. With a passing look at this rich lineage, the discussion highlights how threshold entryways to colonial criminal law required accused subjects to don socially ordered 'masks', or *personas*, when facing its examinations as individuals. Embracing the contingency of such masking, the chapter turns to Naffine's (2003, 2009) analyses of 'legalistic' approaches to persons as historical fictions (rather than metaphysical realities). The analysis then explores the possibility of retelling law's individualising narratives, thus reaching for different legal objects. It alludes to qualitatively different versions of accusation that focus law around collective rather than individual persons, thereby amending its objects and surrounding socio-legal processes. The concluding allusions imply altered incarnations of law, accusation, and different promises of (social) justice.

AN EXAMPLE: CRIMINALLY ACCUSING AN INDIVIDUAL PERSON

On a cold eighth day of February 1883, near of Calgary, a man described as a 'rancher', Joseph Moss, laid an information and complaint to a commissioned justice of the peace, and officer of the NWMP (named McIllree). Less than a decade previously, in 1874, this police force had embarked on a marathon route march from Fort Garry (Winnipeg) to assert its jurisdiction over criminal matters throughout the Dominion defined NWT.[1] Emerging as a colonial institution capable of receiving crime-related information, it 'heard' Moss's accusation that a man named as 'Cutlip' – and described as a 'Sarcee Indian' on the charge form – had stabbed him in the back.[2] The colonial misnaming of Tsuut'ina Nation as 'Sarcee' may reflect a legal requirement to reference a social position without a concomitant obligation to ensure fidelity to those named. Regardless, a month later, McIllree convened a preliminary examination to determine whether there was sufficient evidence to send the matter to trial.[3] Eclipsing long traditions of Indigenous legal pluralism, the Dominion of Canada championed these localised arrangements as *the* legitimate law of the day, thus responding to calls to bring so-called 'civil law' to lands identified for western migration, and to enforce its law on what was misconstrued – given established Indigenous laws (Borrows, 2010) – as a 'lawless' place (W. F. Butler, 1878; Robertson-Ross, 1872). Its rhetoric to 'enforce the law' championed 'European settlement' that by its reasoning meant bringing 'civilization', socio-cultural, and economic 'advancement' (Harring, 2005; Macleod & Rollason, 1997; Nettelbeck et al., 2016; Nevitt & Dempsey, 2010).

One-hundred-and-forty years later, with echoes of Kafka, I sit before an archived instance of that Dominion law, proclaimed through faded scrawls on edge-torn pages. Alert to Derrida's (1996) caveats about the work of governors (*archons*) in what is archived, however, my limited aim is to fuse meaning horizons of now and then as a gesture towards an unfolding political logic; namely, how colonial law's criminalising gaze brought certain accused individuals into focus. Making anachronistic sense of that gaze through a local instance of a preliminary examination, one glimpses contours of a target: an accused person with presumed social ties is called to account as an individual – thus averting legal scrutiny of the dispossessing collective structures that colonial law upheld (Nettelbeck et al., 2016; Pavlich, 2019). The following engagement with an example, then, aims to illustrate how *individually* conceived accused persons, located in social hierarchies, were shaped into being by the preliminary examination of a colonial criminal justice paradigm. Rather than approaching this case as a sampled representation, though there are many similar stories of examinations, the methodology is an interpretative one. Akin to Foucault's (1995) use of the panopticon to signal disciplinary powers, it analyses out of a case (Forrester, 2016) which is viewed as an example of a wider political paradigm (Agamben, 2009). The aim is to engage an unfolding colonial political logic whereby a criminally accused individual could be called to account alone for a criminal act at a gateway to colonial criminalisation. Such a move highlights what Nietzsche called the 'lowly beginnings' of criminal justice, and points to an often-eclipsed politics of accusation that feeds today's vast and unequal crime control arenas (e.g., Alexander, 2010; Cunneen & Tauri, 2016; Monchalin, 2016; Wacquant, 2009).

One might note that despite the grandeur of the rhetoric, the Dominion's political capacity to call subjects to account for crimes rested on the deployment of a few hundred police officers across a vast area of land, spreading from Manitoba to the Rocky Mountains. Even if seldom emphasised, preliminary examinations lay at the centre of its unfolding criminal law. It is here that criminalisation in the name of a colonial sovereign was initiated. So it was that a justice of the peace (McIllree), following an accusation by Moss, claimed a legitimate capacity to call an individual, formally (mis)named as 'Cutlip', to account for 'grievous bodily harm'. Through I did not encounter case records to indicate the accused man's worldviews, one might imagine how his familiar meaning horizons were disrupted as the police arrested him from everyday life, calling him to account as one accused of 'grievous bodily harm' under the omniscient threat of its force – no doubt indicating the complex motivations, from arrest to indictment, by which colonial law's powers swamped his altered world. Furthermore, if the English language spoken was unfamiliar to the accused, the inflected legal idioms might have been even more so; translations too were problematic with radically different vocabularies at play (Harring, 1998).

It was perhaps foreseeable that incoming colonising voices would dominate the examination's legal narrative (the legal authorities and witnesses were not indigenous to the land) with no overt attempts to hear multivocal stories or entertain diverse procedures. A legal guidebook of the day made this clear by requiring justices only to 'hear' and collect evidence by transcribing verbal utterances 'as near as possible in the words of the witness …' (Lewis, 1884, p. 7), and prescribed these procedures:

> After the evidence of a witness has been taken down in writing it should be read over to him and then signed by himself and the Justice or Justices, who shall write (Sworn before me (or us) this day of 188_). before his or their names …. The evidence must be taken in presence of the accused, and he must have an opportunity to ask the witnesses any questions he may think necessary. (Lewis, 1884, p. 7)

Colonial law thus anchored itself to individuals who swore (or in the case of some Indigenous people 'affirm') oaths to tell, 'the whole truth and nothing but the truth, so help you God' (Lewis, 1884, p. 7; see also Clarke, 1872).

On this note, one might recall Foucault's (2014) lectures when thinking about the sort of truth-telling (avowing) demanded by these juridical practices and the limited roles assigned to actors in preliminary examinations. Along these lines, justice McIllree transcribed the accuser Moss's words, under oath, as follows:

> I was coming home to my dinner on Thursday 8th Feb last about 2 pm. When I got in sight of the house … I saw two Indians at the door, one with a white and the other with a black blanket. They appeared to be tampering with the door ….

His archived scrawl relates further that Moss searched the 'prisoner' and found some of his belongings, and that 'the prisoner kept bothering me wanting to shake hands, and I pushed him away from me several times …'. Thereafter, Moss is said to have looked for the 'other Indian' along the river, but was surprised by the accused man:

> I did not hear or see him coming until he stabbed me in the back … he ran with the knife in his hand down the bank. I ran after him until I got too weak to run further … I used no malice towards the prisoner further than by pushing him. The knife was as far as I could judge a larger butcher's knife. I am certain that the prisoner is the man who stabbed me.

The persistent use of the first person in a staccato-like transcription of the accusation alerts us to this law's idioms – genres of storytelling – and how it thereby forged criminally accused persons. To begin with, justices of the peace were obliged to write down the names of subjects who stood before the law, and to describe their social standing as understood by authorised officials. They thereby provided overtones of how to 'read', and what weight to assign to specific people's testimony (see Jones, 1889; McGuire, 1890). So, the examination assigned the name 'Cutlip' to a biopolitically ordered 'Sarcee Indian', while 'Joseph Moss' was economically recognised as a 'rancher'. These nomenclatures probably rang loud cultural bells among local settlers and contoured their perceptions of what veracity weighting to assign to statements made by whom (Harring, 1998; Morgensen, 2011).

Relatedly, and reading between the lines of Moss's information, one can identify injurious conflicts and presumed entitlements as indicated by: a denigrating racism surrounding blinkered references to 'the other Indian'; the arrogance of illicitly searching the accused; a stated and then quickly dismissed allusion to the cultural insult of 'pushing aside' an extended hand of friendship; information that the accused once worked for his accuser; and so on (Byrd, 2011). Simultaneously with allusions to social standing, the accuser, accused, witnesses, and even the mediating justice were framed as individual persons whose delimited stories formed a 'fact-based truth' of unfolding events. The references to the accused's purported social position – names and variously understood social positions – served as a basis for describing different sorts of individual persons as colonial law deemed them to be (Estes, 2020). An overriding logic of this criminal law was then clarified: to assign culpability to an individual person and to divert attention away from the suggestion that imposed colonial relations could be behind conflicts of this kind.

The procedural powers that forged colonial law's individually accused persons through preliminary examinations were buttressed by imputed first- and second-person legal narratives. We can detect elaborate protocols for 'hearing' sworn verbal utterances from single voices, transcribing 'facts', reading them back, signatures and counter signatures (with Xs or not). All insinuated the appearance of a priori individual beings. However, the performances themselves shaped legally recognisable accused individuals – the constructs that it needed to realise its concepts of ordered settlement. In other words, the very demand for responses from individually imagined accusers and accused (and witnesses) forged specific kinds of targets and shaped this law. It was not simply a matter of individuals appearing before a justice, but a more basic coappearance by which persons, processes, and outcome emerged through encounters presented as 'the law'. In this sense too, the unfolding law claimed a monopoly over legal truth. Yet, we should not lose sight of its fictional character, for the colonial craft of law-making was a storytelling instrument: it used legal vocabularies to reduce complex social process to proselytise individualised stories of criminal culpability. Referring to the continued influence of this individualising political logic, Fassin's (2018) analysis of punishment echoes the point:

> Both the liability of the offender and the individualization of the sanction therefore contribute to a narrowing of retribution on the individual held liable, who is deemed solely accountable for the act he allegedly committed and those he might commit in the future. (pp. 109–110)[4]

With that narrowing complex in mind, one might wonder how this law produced the muted voice demanded of its 'accused individuals'. What might 'Cutlip' behind that named mask have experienced as he listened (through translation) to the examination's accusations and witness statements? We cannot know but might point to a long tradition of resistance to such colonial impositions (Estes, 2020). Regardless, contemporary guidebooks for justices did not dwell on such concerns, preferring an emphasis on procedure:

> The information is first read over to the accused, but Justices must bear in mind that this is merely for the purpose of showing the accused what he is charged with .... (Lewis, 1884, p. 7)

At one point, however, McIllree trained his legally authorised gaze squarely upon the accused man, formally recognising – and so shaping – him through an imposed colonial name that also depicted him as an individual person charged with the 'aforementioned crime'. To repeat: this logic categorised him biopolitically (see Morgensen, 2011) as 'a Sarcee Indian', but called him to account alone as a criminally accused individual.

Thus, on a standardised 'Statement of the Accused' form, the justice was required to recognise, name, and so forge, an individual accused of a specifically worded charge or indictment of an offence, with date time, place, and so on. McIllree's charge in this case claimed that, 'Cutlip did attack one Joseph Moss thereby causing grievous bodily harm on the eighth day of February last'. It noted too that 'the said charge' was 'being read to the said Cutlip and the witnesses for the prosecution being so freely examined in his presence' and further that the accused was 'addressed by me as follows: "having heard the evidence do you wish to say anything in answer to the charge? You are not obliged to say anything, unless you desire to do so; but whatever you say will be taken down in writing, and may be given in evidence against you at your trial"'. With that Miranda-like warning, the justice transcribed a translated rendition of what he legally recognised as the accused individual's response, here quoted in full:

> When Moss pushed me over he shaked the knife in pushing me and it cut my leg. This made me mad and I stabbed him in the back. I had been working for Moss, but had not been there for some time when this happened.

This short, transfigured, though rare, glimpse of the accused 'Cutlip's' translated response is revealing. To begin with it calls upon him to account for himself not as a member of the Tsuut'ina Nation, but as 'Cutlip' the individual. Despite his statement's clear counter-accusations of Moss' initial 'cut', or the previous relationship between the men, the justice proceeded as if no statement were heard. And colonial criminal accusations linked an imputed social distinction of personhood (a category of 'Sarcee Indian') to criminal law's demand for a blameworthy, individualised person who could be accused of a crime. To be sure this case may appear to challenge the classifications in *The Indian Act* of 1876 that distinguished, for its purposes, 'persons' from 'Indians', rendering the latter dependents of the state.[5] However, this Act also allowed for different 'constructions' of personhood, enabling this criminal law's claim to jurisdiction over any individual persons who transgressed Dominion defined crimes (Nichols, 2020). Thus, while McIllree's stories made reference to biopolitical distinctions drawn from unfolding social hierarchies of settlement, his examination centred on individually accused persons (as *per* Morgensen, 2011). As such, 'Cutlip' alone was 'Committed to stand trial at the first sitting of the Bow River Court, District no 4'. That judgement followed a contemporary guide by accepting that, 'an old rule of law that prisoners should receive the benefit of every doubt' did not 'apply to examinations' (Lewis, 1884, p. 9).

In short, a colonial political logic at thresholds to local criminalisations fabricated accused individuals out of social distinctions of personhood. They could then be sent to trial and potentially held exclusively culpable for a criminal act ('grievous bodily harm'). A logic that accused singular persons of crimes rendered basic social conflicts, spawned by a local version of colonisation, as unrecogniseable to law. Individuals alone could be held criminally culpable.[6] Returning to Coetzee's story, we might say that by so forging an accused individual at thresholds to criminalisation, colonial criminal law saved itself, and at the same time furthered the immense settlements envisaged by the Dominion it served. That logic has again proved to be historically durable, shaping the way criminal justice continues to operate (Pavlich, 2018). As de Lagasnerie (2018) suggests:

> The system of judgment first deploys an individualizing construction of events. It imputes actions to individuals. Only then can it begin to identify the eventual criminal responsibility of the subject behind the 'criminal act'. (Loc 1035–2693)

But how might we understand the seeming paradox of colonial law recognising social distinctions of personhood while simultaneously calling only accused individual persons to account? In many ways this lands us squarely in a politics of accusation, with malleable forms of legal recognition (Esposito, 2012a, p. 117); but a rich genealogy of legal persons as individuals highlights a wider logic at play.

ACCUSING SOCIALLY LOCATED INDIVIDUALS

One may point to a western politics of accusation that drew upon socio-culturally ideas of personhood to cast criminal law's individual persons (Carrithers, Collins, & Lukes, 1985; Esposito, 2015). This discourse worked out of a politics of masking situated in local, familiar, and assumed social categories. For instance, Roman law recognised ancient masks (*personas*) that symbolised different social privileges and positions accorded to families of standing (Esposito, 2012c, 2015; Parsley, 2010; Supiot, 2017). Such masks were never possessed by individuals, even though,

> every individual was identified by a name that expressed his belonging to a *gens*, to a lineage; but this lineage was defined in turn by the ancestor's mask of wax that every patrician family kept in the atrium of its home. (Agamben, 2011, p. 46)

Moreover, as Supiot (2017, note 69) points out, the life of Roman persons was conditioned by the inheritance of ancestral death masks – the 'imagio' which literally contained the 'imprint of the face of the dead man', a remaining physical or metonymic 'trace of that person'. This mask symbolised a social position that had legal standing. As he explains:

> In Ancient Rome, personality was assigned to the one entrusted with the *imagines* and the names of the ancestors: the *pater familias*. In Roman law, not all human beings had full personality: some were treated as things, while others simply partook of the personality of the *pater familias*. There was no generic concept of 'person' but rather degrees of personality, from slave to *pater familias* via freedmen, free sons and women, peregrines, and so forth. (Supiot, 2017, Kindle Loc 682 of 6991)

Accusation provided a way to connect assigned social positions and criminal law's persons. On the one hand criminal accusations drew upon, 'the place of the individual in the dramas and rituals of social life' (Agamben, 2011, p. 46), and on the other, categorised how individuals alone might be criminalised (Pavlich, 2018, 64ff; Rutledge, 2001). It is worth recalling too that, 'Being a person is anything but a natural given .... No one is born a person' (Esposito, 2012a, p. 116). As such, this lineage echoed a basic element of colonial law; namely, a social hierarchy that permeated colonial distinctions of social persons (Mbembe, 2017). We have alluded to how the Indian Act of 1876 rendered 'Indians' non-persons for its purposes, even though criminal law relied on constructions of Indigenous individuals as subjects who could be accused and held culpable for crimes (Nichols, 2020). We saw too how the accused 'Cutlip' was assigned legal masks that embraced a misnamed distinction of personhood ('Sarcee Indian') even as he faced the law as an individual ('Cutlip') to whom criminal responsibility could be assigned. However, unspoken assumptions about the superiority of settlement, with its 'civilization and progress' narratives, lay behind racially (biopolitically) outlined distinctions of legally accused persons, setting the stage for assigning differential weights to the voices of imagined categories of personhood (Mbembe, 2017).

On this point, colonial legal discourses echoed Roman concerns with social hierarchy, but also a Christian alteration of Roman ladders of personhood which posited the soul as a human reflection of the divine, set against an animalistic body (Esposito, 2012a, p. 21). As Esposito notes, in both modern theological and then enlightenment discourses on personhood, 'Man is a person if and only if he masters the more properly animal part of his nature' (Esposito, 2012c, p. 22). He traces Kant's emphasis on a human capacity to reason as an example of a thought apparatus where mastery of animal natures was thought possible only if individuals embraced their innate powers of reasoning. Overall, though this approach maintains that:

> Man is a person if and only if he masters the more properly animal part of his nature .... Of course not everyone has this tendency or disposition to de-animalize. The degree of humanity present in all will derive from the greater or lesser intensity of de-animalization and ... the underlying difference between he who enjoys the full title of person and he who can enjoy it only if certain conditions have previously been met. (Esposito, 2012a, p. 22)

Such apparatuses reflected a colonial faith that modern, European persons possessed a capacity to 'de-animalize' as individuals with 'civilized' habits (Estes, 2020; Esposito, 2012c, p. 21). When they failed to do so, criminal law was then to enforce civil orders (e.g., W. F. Butler, 1878). As is well known, an imperialist version of this thinking pervaded colonial contexts to imagine degrees of 'de-animalization', and to distinguish supposedly full persons from purportedly lesser persons, especially through distinctions between economically established, and allegedly civilised, settlers, and others (Byrd, 2011; Harring, 1998; Mbembe, 2017). For Esposito, such dynamic relational distinctions of person were not anomalies, but basic to modern conceptions of persons where:

> It isn't possible to personalize someone without depersonalizing or reifying others, without pushing someone over into the indefinite space that opens like a kind a trap door below the person. (Esposito, 2012b, p. 24)

From such ideas one might recall that preliminary examinations imputed different masks or *personas* to participating 'individuals' – one biopolitical

('Sarcee Indian'), the other economic ('rancher'). The designation cast persons on imagined evolutionary ladders of social progress, with certain forms of lives condescendingly cast as closer to animal origins than colonists who were seen as further along with their putative mastery of manners and capitalist occupations (Carter, 1999; Mbembe, 2017; Pavlich, 2014; Tough, 1997). As these blinkered socio-cultural apparatuses accompanied colonial thought, one sees how the accused's voice was weighted differently from a colonising 'rancher' who accused, and why Moss's initial 'cutting' of Cutlip's leg was neither recognised nor pursued as worthy of criminalisation. Moreover, the targeted identity of the accused individual shifted as the preliminary examination unfolded: initially 'Cutlip' was depicted as a 'Sarcee Indian', then as an arrested individual person accused of committing 'grievous bodily harm', and then as an indicted prisoner.

That is, this law conjured a socially located, accused individual into being at the time an information was laid before a police officer. It arrested a familiar life and consigned it temporarily to face the accusations of colonial entrances to criminal law. We should not forget the unequally imposed force behind colonial criminal law's imposition of masks and the indictments that limited an accused's life to the inside of a cell awaiting trial. The criminally accused person was obliged to behave as required under the unspoken threat of force. Subjections of this sort were crucial to 'saving' an individually accused person (as opposed to, say, accusing a dispossessing colonisation), and so saving a specific (colonial) version of criminal law. One might then reiterate our opening sense that the political logic of individualising forms of accusation at thresholds to criminalisation are not superfluous to, but rather at the centre of, historical forms of criminal law. And yet, they are also contingent. Could one recast – or better think about how to recategorise – the criminally accused person at gateways to colonial law? Could we redefine the criminally accused person, recognising that this might require us to recast basic legacies of colonial law, as well as its criminal procedure, rights, duties, obligation, and social imageries?

REVISED LEGAL FICTIONS THAT ACCUSE COLLECTIVE PERSONS

No doubt, such questions echo Esposito's (2015) basic disquiet about western legal persons and an associated quest for a new politics of personhood. Indeed, his intriguing explorations of bodies between persons and things eschews a politics of the personal. One might foreground Esposito's concerns with legal persons by recalling the injustice of Cutlip's prejudicial categorisation as a criminally accused 'Sarcee Indian', but also as an individual, in a preliminary examination that screened out wider colonial power relations. However, one need not share Esposito's (2012a, 2012b, 2012c) faith in an abstracted politics of a 'third person', or of the 'impersonal', or even a Nietzsche-inspired 'affirmative biopolitics' that works over bodies or perhaps 'flesh'. Nor might we accept his panacea-like flight from historically forged immunities envisaged as an elusive politics of impersonality. Perhaps a different politics of categorisation to augment a third-person politics might be summoned to problematise the powers of criminal accusation and its individual persons, thus re-envisioning colonial logics of accusatory categorisation. More directly: instead of seeking an individually accused legal person, might a revised version of law contemplate how to call collective categories of legal persons to account – perhaps thinking through third-person legal arrangements? And what conceptual spur might provide a grounding for such an immense endeavour?

To help here, let us turn to Naffine's (2009) survey of how legal theorists typically approach persons either through 'legalist' or 'metaphysical realist' perspectives. With traces of positivism, formalism, and natural law, these approaches coalesce around responses to two related questions. Should the person be conceived as a way to organise social life and conflict, relying on legal fictions as formal, abstract devices that enable law to specify what kind of beings are to bear its rights, obligations, and duties? Or should law's person reliably locate, capture, and reflect an extra-legal subject as an absolute being depicted (discovered?) by other disciplines (e.g., philosophy, religion, and biology)? Conceived along these lines, Naffine (2009) argues that within legal theory:

> The largest dispute, the biggest intellectual and moral battle, is between those who say that law *does not* and *should not* operate with a natural conception of the person and those who say that it does and should. (p. 20)

She references the former as the 'Legalists' and the latter as 'Metaphysical Realists' who line up behind three camps: 'the Rationalists, Religionists, and Naturalists'. Despite their differences, however, Naffine recognises that the legal person expresses law's jurisdiction (see also Dorsett & McVeigh, 2012).

Her analysis leads to a succinct synopsis:

> Through its concept of the person, law helps to define who matters. The scope and nature of legal personification are both barometers of social and moral thought and the means of practically enforcing those ideas: of giving them the force of law. Law thus absorbs, reflects and expresses ideas in the broader culture about what and who is of value and why. These include religious ideas, philosophical ideas and even scientific ideas. (Naffine, 2009, p. 11)

Without repeating layered discussions of legal persons here (but see Mussawir & Parsley, 2017; Naffine, 2003; Sapontzis, 1981; Thurschwell, 2003; Wishart, 2016), one might develop and extend the 'legalist' sense that persons stem from 'fictions' around which specific forms of law coalesce. We could then approach law's persons as a collective rather than individual fiction, refusing broad liberal attempts to anchor law to essentialised visions of natural, reasonable, free, individual persons (J. P. Butler, 2005; Faguntes, 2000). Rather than searching for a fixed, natural, absolute, or human, person – as a way to restrain socio-political forces from intruding on moral subjects – one might consider new ways to fictionalise the targets of criminal law's gaze, and recalibrate what precisely might count as apposite legal forms to hold that gaze.

The above case shows how a preliminary examination, based on legal fictions of idiomatic transcription, called 'Cutlip' exclusively to account for putatively committing a crime on that cold day. Colonial law's fictional person thus surfaced through stories of a culpable 'individual' – a creation shaped by social categories, bearing the rights and duties stipulated by emerging settler-colonial orders and organised by a justice of the peace (who was also, let us recall, a police officer). Such narratives favoured the accusation of one individual at a time for contravening sovereignly decreed crimes. Of course, such storylines diverted attention away from collective patterns of responsibility. Could another kind of story be told – one that categorises accused persons differently, explicitly recognising surrounding social and power complexes behind relationally moulded patterns of conduct? The complexly of unfolding power arrangements yielded clashes of the sort referenced in our example; these were whittled down through McIlree's legal narratives into a basic transcript. Multifaceted aspects of an event were translated as a criminal accusation, and reduced to determining whether there was enough evidence to hold Cutlip responsible for an alleged offence – a crime that could subsequently be dealt with through the punishment of a culpable individual person.

To put this proposal differently, one might question, extend, and recast the political logic of colonial law's fictional creations of personhood. This questioning could also destabilise the persistence of colonial law by envisaging different ideas of its targeted persons, to address the overlooked racism, prejudice, structured inequality, dispossession, and marginalisation of colonial settlement (Borrows, 2002; Byrd, 2011; Coyle & Borrows, 2017; Napoleon, 2010, 2002). Retelling stories of diverse legal traditions has resurged of late with productive implications for how to rethink relations between common, civil, and Indigenous laws, as well as perhaps notions of citizenship and sovereignty (Asch et al., 2018; Friedland, 2012; Napoleon, 2010; Napoleon & Friedland, 2016; Simpson & Smith, 2014). These ideas may well exceed the present discussion but suggest the value of nurturing alliances with analysts seeking to frame new languages for politics, law, and power (Agamben, 1998; Asch et al., 2018; Brown, 2015; J. P. Butler, 2005). The aim might be to divest legal politics from attachments to individual persons, and to find ways to recalibrate legal objects in pursuit of just relations with others. The issue, that is, lies less with trying to articulate Esposito's post-person legal politics, and more with a socio-cultural reformulation of fictions that cast individuals as the main bearers of law's criminal responsibility. It may also evoke political logics that radically restrict the criminalisation of events, calling for legal responsibility to be focussed on collective relations that produce injurious situations. That is, the aim might be to focus law's gaze on new fictions that cast persons neither as individuals nor fixed beings, but as problematised relations through which destructive forms of association emerge historically.

CONCLUDING ALLUSIONS

What could it mean practically to redirect law's gaze to such collective relations as persons? Consider the archetypal case of stealing a loaf of bread to feed one's family. Is justice better calculated by a law that calls a socially framed 'poor' individual as an accused thief; or could something more be promised by accusing – and so categorising – the unequally social structures that generate poverty and make such actions practicable in certain circumstances? Or to return to our case, could a different sort of law calculate justice not by accusing an Indigenous individual of crime against a 'rancher'? A differently cast law might have directed its gaze to the relational clashes between settlement and dispossession, retelling a fiction of collectively fashioned persons and accusing, say, racist relational contacts, marginalising patterns of settlement, or dispossessing capitalist expansion.

We also have relevant examples internationally, such as in Aotearoa/New Zealand where 'natural features' – for example, the Te Awa Tupua/Whanganui River – have been legally 'recognized as rights-bearing legal persons' (Colwell, Carr-Wilson, & Sandborn, 2017). The aim here is to enable law to respect and recognise environmental, relational, and social harm broadly, and to seek respectful ways of associating and engaging material locations. Or perhaps, transitioning to different modes of accusation, one might point to that country's recent response to the Christchurch massacre. To be sure an individual was incapacitated (with a publication ban), but that reaction was coupled with wider legal responses that categorised collectively imagined targets, such as stricter gun controls, or curbing online violence (Associated Press, 2019; Roy, 2019). I detect here a foreshadowing of different foci for law; namely, collectively imagined fictions that target social relations accused of allowing easy access to automatic weapons, or relations that permit livestreaming of violent acts.

Though there is much to consider in these examples, the general point is whether it might be possible to establish a political logic of accusation that redistributes responsibility to social relations that produce problematic ways of being with others. In other words, might socio-cultural structures that yield problematised economic, social, and cultural expulsions also be cast as legal persons? Could patriarchal and racist relational arrangements, such as those that propel the horrifying proportions of murdered Indigenous women in Canada (Buller et al., 2019), be framed as legal persons, and so worthy of new types of legal gaze? Here, 'the racial state', say, might be understood as a person worthy of legal restraint (Thornton, 2010), presupposing the becoming of new forms of law.

The previous discussion has outlined a colonial political logic that defined criminally accused individuals and located them in social hierarchies via preliminary examinations at the entrances to colonial criminalisation. This political logic, with its long pedigree, involved masking through legal fictions that marked socially located individuals as potentially culpable of committing crime. Questioning this enduring colonial logic, together with the unequal and omniscient criminal justice behemoths it has spawned, this chapter calls for a different legal approach directed at collective persons. The promise is to spread legal responsibility for problematised events to socio-cultural relations that generate them in the first place. It would radically restrict current criminalising processes that deflect attention away from collective accountability by their emphases on individual culpability. It also challenges the cultural life worlds of societies beset by inheritances of an unequal and marginalising colonial criminal law with its individualised crime and punishment narratives. How might new stories refuse the oppressive legacy of a colonial political logic and a criminal law that targets individual persons? Could different calibrations enable new registers of justice, and suggest other calculations of law? Affirmative responses to these questions may be difficult to conceive; but they are vital to shrinking the individually orientated crime control colossi that overwhelm societies born to colonial relational patterns.

ACKNOWLEDGEMENT

The author acknowledges with thanks the insight comments provided through an anonymous review of this chapter.

NOTES

1. Over the years many writers have described and analysed this march and its effects (e.g., see Beal & Macleod, 1984; Foster, 2006; Knafla, 1986; Macleod, 1972, 2000; Marquis, 2006; Nettelbeck et al., 2016, etc.).

2. All references to this case are from the following source: '*The Queen* v. *Cutlip* (Grievous Bodily Harm)', 1883. 78.235/2 Box 2 (Case No. 12). Provincial Archives of Alberta.

3. In this way, Dominion agents claimed exclusive jurisdiction over the Queen's visions of crime, challenging a centuries-old legal pluralism contouring the lands over which it asserted a right to 'settle' (Harring, 1998). The resurgence of Indigenous law, however, indicates the long-term incompleteness of attempts to silence all law in the face of civilising missions (Asch, Borrows, & Tully, 2018; Borrows, 2006; Napoleon, 2010; Napoleon & Friedland, 2016).

4. As Fassin (2018) also notes, modern framings of criminal law's individualised legal persons – whether in settler-colonial or other contexts – were silhouetted against erstwhile collective approaches. Here guilt was: '… inscribed in a process of circulation of persons and goods between clans rather than implying their individual responsibility. The violation of the moral norm or of the social order created a debt that the group had to repay – and not a fault that the individual had to expiate' (p. 48).

5. '12. The term "person" means an individual other than an Indian, unless the context clearly requires another construction ….' From the above, we might note that criminal law was one such context in that Cutlip was required to face its force, just as any other accused person. For the *Indian Act*, however, 'the term Indian' was taken to mean 'First. Any male person of Indian blood reputed to belong to a particular band; Secondly. Any child of such person; Thirdly. Any woman who is or was lawfully married to such person'. For a closer examination of this theme, see Nichols (2020).

6. To be sure, there are instances where corporately framed persons are held to criminal account (e.g., corporations), or where strict or absolute liability cases circumvent ordinary procedures (Vincent, 1989). But in colonial contexts, as now (Duff, 2007), criminal courts assigned responsibility and guilt for crimes to individually framed persons. Lacey's (2015, 2017) work on responsibility attribution calculated through outcomes, characters, actuarial profiles, or psychological personalities may at times suggest a broadening of the logic at work, but notions of the individual person are still basic to such formulations (Esposito, 2012b, 2012c).

REFERENCES

Agamben, G. (1998). *Homo sacer: Sovereign power and bare life*. Stanford, CA: Stanford University Press.

Agamben, G. (2009). *The signature of all things: On method*. New York, NY: Zone Books.

Agamben, G. (2011). *Nudities*. Stanford, CA: Stanford University Press.

Alexander, M. (2010). *The new Jim Crow: Mass incarceration in the age of colorblindness*. New York, NY: New Press.

Antaki, M. (2017). Declining accusation. In G. Pavlich & M. Unger (Eds.), *Accusation: creating criminals* (pp. 44–72). Vancouver: UBC Press.

Asch, M., Borrows, J., & Tully, J. (Eds.). (2018). *Resurgence and reconciliation: Indigenous-settler relations and earth teachings*. Toronto: University of Toronto Press.

Associated Press. (2019). New Zealand MPs overwhelmingly back post-Christchurch gun ban. *The Guardian*, 10 April. Retrieved from https://www.theguardian.com/world/2019/apr/10/new-zealand-mps-overwhelmingly-back-post-christchurch-gun-ban. Accessed on December 5, 2019.

Ayto, J. (2011). *Dictionary of word origins*. New York, NY: Arcade Publishers.

Beal, B., & Macleod, R. C. (1984). *Prairie fire: The 1885 North-West rebellion*. Edmonton: Hurtig.

Borrows, J. (2002). *Recovering Canada: The resurgence of indigenous law*. Toronto: University of Toronto Press.

Borrows, J. (2006). *Indigenous legal traditions in Canada report for the Law Commission of Canada*. Ottawa: Law Commission of Canada.

Borrows, J. (2010). *Canada's indigenous constitution*. Toronto: University of Toronto Press.

Brown, W. (2015). *Undoing the demos: Neoliberalism's stealth revolution*. New York, NY: Zone Books.

Buller, M. et al. (2019). Reclaiming power and place: The final report of the national inquiry into missing and murdered indigenous women and girls. Retrieved from https://www.mmiwg-ffada.ca/final-report/. Accessed on December 20, 2019.

Butler, J. P. (2005). *Giving an account of oneself* (4th ed.). New York, NY: Fordham University Press.

Butler, W. F. (1878). *The great lone land: A narrative of travel and adventure in the north-west of America*. London: S. Low, Marston, Searle & Rivington.

Byrd, J. A. (2011). *The transit of empire: Indigenous critiques of colonialism*. Minneapolis, MN: University of Minnesota Press.

Carrithers, M., Collins, S., & Lukes, S. (1985). *The category of the person: Anthropology, philosophy, history*. Cambridge: Cambridge University Press.

Carter, S. (1999). *Aboriginal people and colonizers of western Canada to 1900. Themes in Canadian social history*. Toronto: University of Toronto Press.

Clarke, S. R. (1872). *A treatise on criminal law as applicable to the Dominion of Canada*. Toronto: Carswell.

Coetzee, J. M. (2016). The Schooldays of Jesus. London: Penguin (Kindle Edition).

Colwell, R., Carr-Wilson, S., & Sandborn, C. (2017). *Legal personality of natural features*. Wellington: Victoria University of Wellington.

Coyle, M., & Borrows, J. (Eds.). (2017). *The right relationship: Reimagining the implementation of historical treaties*. Toronto: University of Toronto Press.

Cunneen, C., & Tauri, J. (2016). *Indigenous criminology*. Bristol: Policy Press.

de Lagasnerie, G. (2018). *Judge and punish: The penal state on trial*. Stanford, CA: Stanford University Press.

Derrida, J. (1996). *Archive fever: A Freudian impression*. Chicago, IL: University of Chicago Press.

Dorsett, S., & McVeigh, S. (2012). *Jurisdiction*. New York, NY: Routledge-Cavendish.

Duff, R. A. (2007). *Answering for crime: Responsibility and liability in the criminal law*. Oxford: Hart Publishing.

Esposito, R. (2012a). *Terms of the political: Community, immunity, biopolitics*. New York, NY: Fordham University Press.

Esposito, R. (2012b). The dispositif of the person. *Law, Culture and the Humanities*, *8*(1), 17–30. https://doi.org/10.1177/1743872111403104

Esposito, R. (2012c). *Third person: Politics of life and philosophy of the impersonal*. Cambridge: Polity Press.

Esposito, R. (2015). *Persons and things: From the body's point of view*. Cambridge: Polity Press.

Estes, N. (2020). *Our history is the future: Standing rock versus the Dakota access pipeline, and the long tradition of indigenous resistance*. New York, NY: Verso.

Faguntes, D. (2000). What we talk about when we talk about persons: The language of a legal fiction. *Harvard Law Review*, *114*, 1746.

Fassin, D. (2018). *The will to punish*. Oxford: Oxford University Press.

Forrester, J. (2016). *Thinking in cases*. Cambridge: Polity Press.

Foster, H. (2006). Law and necessity in western Rupert's land and beyond, 1670–1870. In L. A. Knafla & J. Swainger (Eds.), *Laws and societies in the Canadian Prairie West, 1670–1940* (pp. 70–91). Vancouver: UBC Press.

Foucault, M. (1995). *Discipline and punish: The birth of the prison* (2nd Vintage Books). New York, NY: Vintage Books.

Foucault, M. (2014). *Wrong-doing, truth-telling: The function of avowal in justice*. Chicago, IL: University of Chicago Press.

Friedland, H. (2012). Reflective frameworks: Methods for accessing, understanding and applying indigenous laws. *Indigenous Law Journal, 11*(1), 1–40.

Harring, S. L. (1998). *White man's law: Native people in nineteenth-century Canadian jurisprudence*. Toronto: University of Toronto Press.

Harring, S. L. (2005). "There seemed to be no recognized law": Canadian law and the Prairie first nations. In *Laws and societies in the Canadian Prairie West, 1670–1870*. Vancouver: UBC Press.

Jones, J. T. (1889). *Magistrates' manual; or, handy book compiled from the revised criminal law, revised statutes of Canada, and revised statutes of Ontario, 1887, with the several amendments made thereto*. Toronto: Carswell.

Knafla, L. A. (Ed.). (1986). *Law and justice in a new land: Essays in western Canadian legal history*. Toronto: Carswell.

Lacey, N. (2015). Socializing the subject of criminal law: Criminal responsibility and the purposes of criminalization. *Marquette Law Review, 99*, 541.

Lacey, N. (2017). *In search of criminal responsibility: Ideas, interests, and institutions*. Oxford: Oxford University Press.

Lewis, E. N. (1884). *A manual containing a short summary of the usual practice and manner of proceeding in ordinary cases coming under the observation of justices of the peace: Coroners, constables, landlords, bailiffs, etc*. Toronto: Carswell.

Macleod, R. C. (1972). *The north-west mounted police 1873–1905: Law enforcement and the social order in the Canadian North-West*. Toronto: University of Toronto Press.

Macleod, R. C. (2000). Canada's mounties: Myth and reality. *History Today*, February, pp. 39–44.

Macleod, R. C., & Rollason, H. (1997). "Restrain the lawless savages": Native defendants in the criminal courts of the North West Territories, 1878–1885. *Journal of Historical Sociology, 10*(2), 157–83. https://doi.org/10.1111/1467-6443.00035

Marquis, G. (2006). Policing two imperial frontiers: The royal Irish constabulary and the north-west mounted police. In L. A. Knafla and J. Swainger (Eds.), *Laws and societies in the Canadian Prairie West, 1670–1940* (pp. 185–210). Vancouver: UBC Press.

Mbembe, A. (2017). *Critique of black reason*. Durham: Duke University Press.

McGuire, T. H. (1890). *A handbook for magistrates in relation to summary convictions and orders and indictable offences*. Toronto: Carswell.

Monchalin, L. (2016). *The colonial problem: An indigenous perspective on crime and injustice in Canada*. Toronto: University of Toronto Press.

Morgensen, S. L. (2011). The biopolitics of settler colonialism: Right here, right now. *Settler Colonial Studies, 1*(1), 52–76. https://doi.org/10.1080/2201473X.2011.10648801

Mussawir, E., & Parsley, C. (2017). The law of persons today: At the margins of jurisprudence. *Law and Humanities, 11*(1), 44–63. https://doi.org/10.1080/17521483.2017.1320041

Naffine, N. (2003). Who are law's persons? From cheshire cats to responsible subjects. *Modern Law Review, 66*(3), 346–67. https://doi.org/10.1111/1468-2230.6603002

Naffine, N. (2009). *Law's meaning of life: Philosophy, religion, Darwin, and the legal person*. Legal Theory Today. Oxford: Hart Pub.

Napoleon, V. (2002). Raven's garden: A discussion about aboriginal sexual orientation and transgender issues. *Canadian Journal of Law and Society, 17*(02), 149–71. https://doi.org/10.1017/S0829320100007286

Napoleon, V. (2010). Behind the blockades. *Indigenous Law Journal, 9*(1), 1–15.

Napoleon, V., & Friedland, H. (2016). An inside job: Engaging with indigenous legal traditions through stories. *McGill Law Journal, 4*(1), 725–745.

Nettelbeck, A., Smandych, R., Knafla, L. A., & Foster, R. (2016). *Fragile settlements: Aboriginal peoples, law, and resistance in South-West Australia and Prairie Canada*. Vancouver: UBC Press.

Nevitt, R. B., & Dempsey, H. (2010). *Frontier life in the mounted police: The diary letters of Richard Barrington Nevitt, NWMP Surgeon, 1874–1878*. Historical Society of Alberta (vol. XVIII). Calgary: Alberta Records Publication Board, Historical Society of Alberta.

Nichols, J. B. D. (2020). *A reconciliation without recollection?: An investigation of the foundations of aboriginal law in Canada*. Toronto: University of Toronto Press.

Parsley, C. (2010). The mask and Agamben: The transitional juridical technics of legal relation. *Law Text Culture, 14*, vii.

Pavlich, G. (2014). Criminal justice and Cape law's persons. *Social & Legal Studies, 23*(1), 55–72. https://doi.org/10.1177/0964663913502509

Pavlich, G. (2018). *Criminal accusation: Political rationales and socio-legal practices*. New York, NY: Routledge.

Pavlich, G. (2019). Accusatory entryways to criminal justice. In G. Pavlich & M. Unger (Eds.), *Entryways to criminal justice: Accusation and criminalization in Canada* (pp. 1–28). Edmonton: University of Alberta Press.

Robertson-Ross, P. (1872). *Report on Colonel Robertson-Ross, adjt.-general of militia, on the north-west provinces and territories of the Dominion*. Ottawa: Government Printers.

Roy, E. A. (2019). Christchurch call: Details emerge of Ardern's plan to tackle online extremism. *The Guardian*, May 13. Retrieved from https://www.theguardian.com/world/2019/may/13/christch-urch-call-details-emerge-of-arderns-plan-to-tackle-online-extremism Accessed on June 12, 2019.

Rutledge, S. H. (2001). *Imperial inquisitions: Prosecutors and informants from Tiberius to Domitian*. New York, NY: Routledge.

Sapontzis, S. F. (1981). A critique of personhood. *Ethics, 91*(4), 607–618.

Simpson, A., & Smith, A. (Eds.). (2014). *Theorizing native studies*. Durham: Duke University Press.

Supiot, A. (2017). *Homo juridicus: On the anthropological function of the law*. London: Verso.

Thornton, M. (2010). The racial state as legal person. *Australian Journal of Legal Philosophy, 35*, 140.

Thurschwell, A. (2003). Specters of Nietzsche: Potential futures for the concept of the political in Agamben and Derrida. *Cardozo Law Review, 24*, 1193–1259.

Tough, F. (1997). *As their natural resources fail: Native peoples and the economic history of northern Manitoba, 1870–1930*. Vancouver: UBC Press.

Veracini, L. (2014). Understanding colonialism and settler colonialism as distinct formations. *Interventions, 16*(5), 615–633. https://doi.org/10.1080/1369801X.2013.858983

Vincent, A. (1989). Can groups be persons?. *The Review of Metaphysics, 42*(4), 687–715.

Wacquant, L. (2009). *Punishing the poor: The neoliberal government of social insecurity*. Durham: Duke University Press.

Wishart, D. (2016). Puzzling out law's person. *Indiana Journal of Global Legal Studies, 23*, 743–750.

CHAPTER 2

GITXSAN LEGAL PERSONHOOD: GENDERED

Val Napoleon[1]

ABSTRACT

In this chapter, the author explores the conditions of sexualised, gendered violence against Indigenous women and girls. The author asks how various responses to this violence have shaped the present-day legal personhood of Indigenous women and girls from two perspectives: an Indigenous legal perspective and a Canadian legal perspective. To avoid the troublesome pan-Indigenous generalisations of legal personhood, the author focusses on one Indigenous society, the Gitxsan people from northwest British Columbia and their legal order and laws.[2] *The author examines several specific questions about how the Gitxsan legal tradition historically defined the legal personhood of Gitxsan women and girls, and how this has changed with colonisation. The author takes up specific aspects of the operation and structure of Gitxsan law and legal institutions and analyse the ways that they are gendered.*

Keywords: Indigenous legal methodologies; Indigenous feminism; Indigenous personhood; Indigenous law and legal theories; Indigenous narratives/oral histories; law and gender

CONTEXT

Her name was Cindy Gladue, 'not "native woman"', and the Supreme Court of Canada says that in future, trial judges 'would be well advised to provide an express instruction (for

Interrupting the Legal Person
Studies in Law, Politics, and Society, Volume 87A, 19–32

Published under exclusive licence by Emerald Publishing Limited
ISSN: 1059-4337/doi:10.1108/S1059-43372022000087A002

juries) aimed at countering prejudice against Indigenous women and girls' like her. (Christie Blatchford, May 24, 2019, *National Post*)

Is there justice for Indigenous women who have been sexually assaulted in Canada? … The case is about Cindy Gladue, a victim of sexual violence who bled to death in a hotel bathtub. In its decision, the court found that Bradley Barton, the accused, had lied, destroyed evidence and admitted that he caused Ms Gladue's death. He was acquitted at trial. The Alberta Court of Appeal overturned the acquittal and ordered a new trial for murder and manslaughter. The SCC also ordered a new trial, but only for manslaughter.

Ms Gladue was an Indigenous woman and a sex worker. She paid for both of these facts with her privacy, her dignity and her life. The case is known by her name, as if she was the one on trial. And naming is important. It reveals how we understand what we are viewing. In this case, the naming is, sadly, accurate. It was Ms Gladue's life and body that were on trial.

Ms. Gladue paid another new and shocking price in this trial: The Crown brought part of her preserved pelvic [vaginal] tissue into the courtroom, as evidence of the wound she suffered. She was literally made an object, called a specimen and tissue. Further, there were more than 50 references to her in the trial as 'native' and 'prostitute.' She was robbed of her humanity. (Jean Teillet, May 27, 2019, *Globe and Mail*)

INTRODUCTION

In Canada and elsewhere in the world, there is a societal scale failure to ascribe political and legal meaning to the decisions and actions of Indigenous women and girls. This is the case both before and after their deaths. Against this distressing but real backdrop, what does agency mean for Indigenous women and girls? How and why does their agency matter? I am using the term 'agency' to mean the capacity of Indigenous women and girls to act – capacity of will, mind, spirit, and humanity. This is personhood in its fullest possible conception. We have a failure to recognise the agency of Indigenous women and girls. And we have denial. It is the very denial of Indigenous women and girls' agency that fosters and enables the relentless sexist dehumanisation and ultimately, dangerous disposability of Indigenous women and girls.[3]

What is our perspective of the over 4,000 missing and murdered Indigenous women and girls when we do not take their agency and political circumstances into account? What kind of understanding do we have of the violence against Indigenous women and girls when we do not factor in the combined political, social, and economic conditions that generate the racialised and sexualised violence against them? Extensively documented by the Canadian state and others, many Indigenous communities in both rural and urban settings, face debilitating conditions of violence such as poverty, political and economic marginalisation, racialisation, lack of education and employment, poor or limited housing, poor health, lack of safe drinking water, and high incarceration levels. My starting place is that the missing and murdered Indigenous women and girls in Canada (and elsewhere in the world) are legal agents, persons, and citizens who made the best decisions they could within and against the constraints of the power relations that they are a part of and which surrounded them.

When we take up the perspectives of Indigenous women and girls, we are according them the ability to reason, to assess, and to make decisions within their own lives. What quickly becomes obvious, given the conditions, is that there are no margins for error or crisis (e.g., the kids need new shoes or school supplies), and that one has less power in relation to landlords, government social workers, police, and others. Life decisions then are made when there is little money and often fear and addictions. Where we are located in the surrounding relations of power is determinative of the reach of our decisions (i.e., what we can realistically change) and of the logic of those decisions (i.e., putting our own safety at risk). Failure to see the agency of women and girls, or the societally caused conditions of violence, makes it possible to only see them as victims or even, as deserving of their fates.

Over the years, I have asked students and various audiences to imagine the missing and murdered Indigenous women and girls as legal agents, persons, and citizens operating within and through their surrounding power relations. I would then ask whether and how this additional lens influenced or changed their understanding of the missing and murdered women and girls. Sometimes my question made no difference as the assumptions about Indigenous women and girls were just too deeply entrenched and were therefore unquestionable. For example, about 15 years ago, in response to my question, I was told by a young non-Indigenous woman from a feminist law students group, that the missing and murdered Indigenous women and girls were sex trade workers – full stop – and therefore were no concern of theirs. According to these very privileged students, there was no 'issue' of missing and murdered women, not one that mattered to their version of feminism anyway.[4] Others, however, admitted that my question created a kind of uncomfortable cognitive dissonance for them because their brains had difficulty holding the two contradictory ideas of 'victim' versus 'agent' at once, and this caused each to keep cancelling the each other out. Mine was an intentional disruption of the public imagination which too often pathologises Indigenous women and girls into one-dimensional victims that made poor individual lifestyle choices and whose communities are inherently violent.

In this chapter, I want to explore how the combined conditions of violence as well as the various responses to this sexualised, gendered violence, have shaped the present day legal personhood of Indigenous women and girls from an Indigenous legal perspective and from a Canadian legal perspective. To avoid pan-Indigenous generalisations of legal personhood, I will focus on the Gitxsan legal order and laws. I will explore how law operates through Gitxsan institutional forms, and I will apply a gendered analysis. With this aim, I will examine several specific questions about how the Gitxsan legal tradition historically defined the legal personhood of Gitxsan women and girls, and whether and how this has changed with colonisation. To do this, I will take up specific aspects of the operation and structure of Gitxsan law and legal institutions to explore the ways that they are gendered in practice. This small exploration will include rights and rights bearers, individual and collective culpability and liability, marriage and divorce, and leadership considerations.

For this chapter, my approach to Gitxsan law is informed by legal scholar, Kristen Rundle, and her rich interpretation and development of Lon Fuller's legal theory (Rundle, 2012). According to Rundle (2019, p. 19), 'analysis, procedures, and institutional forms … are vehicles for the carriage of governing relationships [because] they carry the responsibilities and opportunities of the authority of law itself'. Rundle helpfully argues that these relational demands are constitutive of Fuller's legalities, and further that they apply beyond state law's legislative mode of governance to all governing relationships framed by law and this would include non-state Gitxsan law.

GITXSAN LEGAL PERSONHOOD

Located in northwest British Columbia, the Gitxsan were one of the plaintiff groups in the seminal Aboriginal title action at the Supreme Court of Canada action, *Delgamuukw*.[5] Gitxsan society is non-state with horizontal, decentralised structuring of its economic, political, social, and legal institutions. In other words, there were no separate centralised or hierarchical bureaucracies delegated with the responsibility for governance and law. So, in Gitxsan society, what is the Gitxsan legal imaginary of personhood? According to Gitxsan law (historic and present), only a Gitxsan person or legal personality has rights, protections, privileges, responsibilities, and legal liability.[6]

So historically, how might women and girls have understood themselves as legal persons in Gitxsan society in accordance with Gitxsan law? And today, how might women and girls understand themselves in accordance with Gitxsan law? Obviously as with every other society, Gitxsan women and girls would have understood, and do understand themselves in relation to how Gitxsan society was organised and how that normative order actually operated in and through their lives (Napoleon, 2009; Overstall, 2005).

Around Gitxsan women and girls, there is a complex network of kinship relationships each formed by and containing legal, economic, and political obligations that comprise Gitxsan governance. Within this relational complex, Gitxsan women and girls have defined obligations to others, and, in turn, there are similar obligations that those others hold to them. Political and legal authorities operated and still operate through matrilineal kinship units that share a common ancestry called the House in English.[7] It is the House that is the land and fishing site owning entity, and there is no higher political or legal authority than the House in Gitxsan society. In turn, all the Houses are divided into four clans which operate as alliances for broader economic, political, and legal purposes.

Since Gitxsan society is matrilineal and every person (male, female, or other) is born into their mother's House, women and girls would know that their own children's House membership also derives through them. In other words, their children and their sisters' children, and the children of other female House members would form and be responsible to the same kinship unit and its governance, be part of the collective ownership of the same territories, be legally and politically defined by the same oral histories,[8] be entitled to the same privileges and prerogatives, and be subject to their House obligations and liabilities. In contrast, men and boys would know that they belong to their mother's House, and their own children will belong to their own mother's House.

Houses that did not have enough women and girls would shrink in size meaning that the unit would have great difficulty upholding its legal, political, and economic obligations to the land, the House, and to other Houses. The options would be to adopt women and girls from other Houses or combine with another House for as along as their numbers were low. Gitxsan legal personhood for women and girls begins with these embodied constructs which are central to the continuation of the identity, strength, and health of Gitxsan governance, legal order, and economy. However, if one's mother was not Gitxsan but one's father was, one would have to be adopted in according to Gitxsan citizenship law, usually by his or her spouse's father's House. This adoption would enable one to be a member of a House with the ability to operate fully within Gitxsan society. Without this membership, one would not be considered Gitxsan.[9]

Within the House, through their respective female lineages, women and girls comprise the House entity itself, along with their brothers and male relatives. House members are individual legal agents within their House. However, beyond the House, it is the House entity that is the collective legal agent in the overall system, so it is the House that relates to other Houses for all collective House business. Gitxsan legal personhood means that women and girls would understand themselves both as individual legal agents within their House and as part of an active legal collective beyond their House.

The next level of citizenship forming the legal personhood of Gitxsan women and girls is at the clan level as each House in turn forms one of the four clans, a larger political collective. Women and girls would understand themselves in this larger clan framework and it is the clan which forms the basis for and primary connection to neighbouring peoples such as the Haida, Haisla, Nisga'a, Wet'suwet'en, or Tsimshian, for instance.[10] Here, women would understand their relationships to contain both obligations and rights through their Houses and clans to equivalent lineages from neighbouring peoples, the Nisga'a and Gitxsan, and others.

Gitxsan society is exogamous requiring marriage outside one's clan, and historically, marriages (i.e., heterosexual) were arranged (Napoleon, 2002). While still being concerned with the economic well-being of their husbands' Houses, women would have maintained separate economic lives because their husbands belonged to a House from a different clan with its own territories. For women, their participation in the arranged marriages was necessary to the political and economic health of their House for a host of reasons including territory location and adjacency, political alliances, trade relations, or conflict management (Napoleon, 2009). However, despite the importance of their marriages, women (and men) were also entitled to no fault divorce, and each woman could publicly initiate and complete her divorce proceedings with the support of her House.[11] Gitxsan women had a right to a residence either in their mother's village or by arrangement, in their husband's village.

Today, while marriages are no longer arranged, one is heavily discouraged from marrying within one's clan. Though not about bloodlines, marriages within the same clan was sometimes described in English as incestuous, and such problematic and shameful marriages would have to be rectified through adoption[12] of either the husband or wife into a House from another clan, usually to one of their paternal Houses. The concerns here are economic as well as political because the mother's lineage and the father's lineage have different legal duties to each House member, and they take up different economic roles and responsibilities in the Feast hall. In some situations, despite corrective adoptions, there are ongoing tensions and disapproval that continue to play out between Houses and between members today as in the past.

Gitxsan women and girls have access to various House territories. First through their mother's lineage, they have access to their own House territories. Second, through specific and bounded agreements, women and girls have access to their father's House territories, and it is also possible to arrange access to their spouse's territory. The House territories are held in trust by the House chiefs, in the name of the House chief (I will expand on this a little further below).

Each House owns and has authority and responsibility for a number of chiefly names – a head chief name and wing chiefs' names, and each name indicates the status of those members in the House.[13] While the names form part of the intellectual property of each House, more importantly, they comprise and form the decentralised Gitxsan governance structure.[14] Some women are able increase their status and authority through obtaining chief names, no easy undertaking and a serious accomplishment. Women also advocate on many levels to secure recognition for their children in the Gitxsan political structure because obtaining political recognition and names is a highly competitive process.

Each House also has independent *nax nox,* spiritual relations that are not connected with territory and crests. The chiefs bring these spiritual relations to life by their nax nox performances at the Feasts. The nax nox performances are considered property of the House (Overstall, 2005, p. 29) and the chiefly names are infused with specific nax nox powers that become part of the chiefs who hold them. According to anthropologist Susan Marsden (2008):

> The chief, in controlling one of these forces, takes on its name as one of his own. If the person taking a *naxnox* name is not sufficiently strong, the spirit force in the name controls him [or her] and he himself [she herself] becomes restless, thoughtless, or stupid.[15]

In other words, a legal person who is also a chief, must maintain their authority by publicly withstanding and overcoming weaknesses that are personified in the nax nox. Several of the newer nax nox include cigarette smoking and drinking alcohol while other older nax nox include natural phenomenon (e.g., whirlwinds), laziness, sleepiness, and so on.

Historically, Gitxsan women and girls could have been victims of violence, including sexual violence, from surrounding peoples (Cove & MacDonald, 1987a, 1987b).[16] If they were kidnapped, they had a right to be redeemed by the Gitxsan unless they chose not to be.[17] In the event of kidnapping it would have been possible for women and girls to maintain their rank in that other society.

However, if women were seriously harmed, including by another Gitxsan citizen, they had a right to legal action and compensation which would have been acted on by their mother's House with support by their father's side. Historically, women, as with others who are injured or wronged, had a right to equal negotiation with the offender, they were not sidelined as victims in this process. What is critical here is that since there are no legal professionals or centralised bureaucracy of law, women are, to varying degrees, responsible for knowing and maintaining the Gitxsan legal order.

In short, women were and are part of number of legal Gitxsan collectivities in which they had responsibilities and legal obligations, and they had similar responsibilities and legal obligations owing to them. Historically and to varying degrees today, women would have had recourse to Gitxsan law in the event of conflicts or injury, and they have a right to participating directly in negotiating their compensation. While it is true that women's status within Gitxsan society could vary depending on a number of factors, it is also true that they had fairly high level of mobility, authority, and autonomy within their society.

SOME OF THE COLONIAL EROSION

Gitxsan women and girls have experienced the establishment of small reserves and the prohibition of political activities through the imposition of the federal *Indian Act* (R.S.C. 1985, c. 1-5). These reserves are a tiny fragment of the Gitxsan historic territories and they served to fracture the larger legal order, economy, and governing system. Despite Canadian prohibitions, Gitxsan people continued to secretly act on their land ownership obligations through the Feast system, but their ability to generate wealth to maintain their economy was almost destroyed. Nonetheless, when the Canadian law prohibiting potlatches was lifted, there was some disconnection between Gitxsan people's continued public fulfilment of legal obligations required by Gitxsan land and governance laws through the institution of the Feast, and their actual ability to protect their collectively owned lands, to enforce laws, and to manage and harvest their resources. There are many reasons for this continued disabling of Gitxsan law including third party settler lands, imposition of federal and provincial jurisdictions, and industrial resource extraction activities.

Women's political consciousness would have been reoriented inward to within reserve boundaries, and away from a political consciousness that would have included territories and other Indigenous peoples that they are connected to. Those that are accountable to women under Gitxsan law and those that they are accountable to could very likely belong to a different band and residing on a separate reserve, and consequently their ability to act fully as legal agents in Gitxsan law has been undermined.

Women and girls were not and are not active legal agents in the Canadian laws that shaped their lives or experiences such as the *Indian Act*. Under Canadian law, they were not able to decide where they could live, obtain a divorce as easily as in the past, or choose who to affiliate with. Women had virtually no protection from Canadian law in the event of harm or injury from anyone. They would not have the economic security afforded to them through the kinship system and collective land ownership. For much of this early time with the *Indian Act*, women were not able to run for the newly imposed and established political structures like the band council. Only 'Indian' men could vote in Indian band business or elections, and only males could hold office on reserve under the *Indian Act* (1876, s. 61), a regime that lasted until 1951. Outside the reserve, neither Indigenous men or women were able to vote provincially or federally until 1951 (Napoleon, 2001).[18]

However, despite early colonial history, today Gitxsan women and girls still understand themselves as part of a lineage that has historic connections to certain lands, they continue to participate in feasts and other legal events, they continue to have their children follow their lineage, and they still advocate for the recognition of their children in the Gitxsan system. We can see that their experiences would depend on where they live – whether in Gitxsan territory or elsewhere in the world, whether on-reserve or off-reserve, and in which Gitxsan community. Each situation creates different issues and potentially different experiences. Today, Gitxsan women are still navigating an enormously complex lawscape of competing legal orders, and they are managing themselves within both Gitxsan law and Canadian law – with all the attendant tensions and conflicts. The operation and imposition of patriarchal settler law not only undermined Gitxsan women and girls in their lives, it also disrupted the lawful gender roles and relations and in doing so destabilised the function and practice of Gitxsan law at every level – personal, family, extended family, and beyond.

MISSING AND MURDERED INDIGENOUS WOMEN AND GIRLS

There is no room for idealisation or romanticism when it comes to violence against Indigenous women and girls, and historically, Gitxsan people were no more violent or sexist than any other society (Snyder, Napoleon, & Borrows, 2015). However, as with other Indigenous women and girls in Canada and elsewhere, Gitxsan women and girls experienced gendered and sexual violence in the past as many of the oral histories attest to. Today, there is shameless, normalised sexism in Gitxsan and in other Indigenous communities, and the violence against Gitxsan women and girls is at the same appalling high rate as elsewhere.

What is important is to understand here is that violence happens in spaces of 'lawlessness'. While violence obviously also happens in spaces of lawfulness, for my purposes here, Indigenous lawlessness is created in two ways: (i) the undermining of Indigenous law and the creation of gaps and distortions in Indigenous lawfulness, and (ii) the failure of Canadian law to protect Indigenous women and girls. One example is that the over 40 Indigenous women and girls who disappeared or were murdered on the northern 'Highway of Tears' which crosses Gitxsan territories, included Gitxsan women and girls. According to a Human Rights Watch (2013) report:

> The province of British Columbia has been particularly badly affected by violence against indigenous women and girls and by the failure of Canadian law enforcement authorities to deal with the phenomenon. Cutting through the small communities policed by the Royal Canadian Mounted Police (RCMP) in northern BC is the Highway of Tears, a 724-kilometer stretch of road which has become infamous for the dozens of women and girls who have gone missing or been murdered in its vicinity.

> …
>
> The failure of law enforcement authorities to deal effectively with the problem of missing and murdered indigenous women and girls in Canada is just one element of the dysfunctional relationship between the Canadian police and indigenous communities. This report addresses the relationship between the RCMP and indigenous women and girls in northern BC and documents not only how indigenous women and girls are under-protected by the police but also how some have been the objects of outright police abuse.

There have been numerous inquiries into the violence against Indigenous women leading one group to call their report, *Researched to Death: B.C. Aboriginal Women and Violence* (Ending Violence Association BC, 2005). The most recent national inquiry report, *Reclaiming Power and Place: The Final Report of the National Inquiry into Missing and Murdered Indigenous Women and Girls* (National Inquiry into Missing and Murdered Indigenous Women and Girls, 2019b), is the largest undertaking comprising three years of hearings with testimony from 2,380 family members and experts, and 231 calls to justice aimed at governments, institutions, social service providers, industries, and all Canadians.

It is no surprise that Indigenous women and girls are subjects of numerous studies. *Reclaiming Power and Place: The Final Report of the National Inquiry into Missing and Murdered Indigenous Women and Girls* (National Inquiry into Missing and Murdered Indigenous Women and Girls, 2019b) is well over 1,200 pages in length and has already generated much controversy over its use of the term genocide to frame the gendered violence it documents. The report will provide a useful resource for years to come as have previous volumes published by the large national commissions, the Canadian Truth and Reconciliation Commission and the Royal Commission of Canada. While the *National Inquiry into Missing and Murdered Indigenous Women and Girls* final report (2019a) does provide a discussion of Indigenous law and gender, its main focus is on describing the continued experience of colonialism, the failure of the Canadian legal system including law enforcement, and rights to culture, health, security, and justice. This is not surprising given its mandate to report on the systemic causes of all forms of violence, and institutional policies and practices in response to violence experienced by Indigenous (First Nations, Métis, and Inuit) women and girls[19] in Canada.

What can we learn from this report about how the legal personhood of Indigenous women and girls is defined? The report basically locates Indigenous women and girls within the Canadian legal, economic, and political systems – and for the most part, the calls to justice are addressed to institutions outside of Indigenous societies and communities. It is difficult to say what Indigenous women and girls' legal personhood is at this point, as what will be telling and definitive is whether the report's calls to justice are acted on or enforced.

According to this report, the rights that Indigenous women and girls have, including human rights and self-determination rights, are located outside Indigenous law and do not derive from within Indigenous legal traditions. While the report speaks to the importance of relationships, the recommendations do not address Indigenous communities or an Indigenous legal response (National Inquiry into Missing and Murdered Indigenous Women and Girls, 2019a, pp. 10–12).

The work of Indigenous scholars Heidi Kiiwetinepinesiik Stark and Gina Starblanket (2018) is important to consider here in order to get at the complexity of acting on relationality and its requirements for healthy relationships (p. 121):

> The idea here is that the reconnection of people with one another, and of individuals and the land isn't necessarily transformative in and of itself, but that it is the proliferation of relationships of care and nurturance, in which we see ourselves having concrete roles and responsibilities that have the greatest promise.
>
> Imagine the transformations that could occur when humans begin to realize that we are not neutral in the face of crises that surround us, but instead recognize that through our choices we have the potential to actively change the world we inhabit.

Kiiwetinepinesiik Stark and Starblanket carefully locate the responsibility and potential for responding to crisis through our relationships, and in doing so, they are suggesting that Indigenous peoples have the agency to determine what kind of response to make. In the work that I am currently engaged in with the Indigenous Law Research Unit located at the University of Victoria, we are researching and restating human rights from an internal Indigenous legal perspective, that is, from within Indigenous legal traditions.[20] For example, how does Gitxsan law construct dignity, agency, and safety for Gitxsan women? It is my position that this direction into the work of Indigenous law is essential if any real change is to be wrought for and with Indigenous women.

All law, including Gitxsan law, are constituting of and constituted by surrounding power dynamics. Sexism and gendered violence have always been legal issues for Gitxsan law, and this reality is affirmed by the oral histories. Given this, some of the Gitxsan human rights research questions are: (i) How do gendered power dynamics shape Gitxsan legal interpretations today? (ii) What are the Gitxsan legal principles concerning gender? (iii) What assumptions are being made about the ways that gendered subjects engage with Gitxsan law, and why? (iv) How are governance and property laws gendered?

CONCLUSION

Every legal tradition holds both its promise and its potential of failure, and Gitxsan law is no exception. One can see from the very short description of Gitxsan legal institutions that Gitxsan society has the clear potential to be non-sexist as it is matrilineal, and the complex of governing relations enable individual and collective inclusion, accountability, and responsibilities. Arguably, the same can be said about the potential of Canadian law, or even about democracy itself. However, we also know that both Canadian law and democracy are fraught with racism and sexism, and there are ongoing struggles and oppressions. As with other societies, Gitxsan oral histories illustrate that gendered and sexual violence have always been a struggle, and Gitxsan people have always had to have law to deal with it. Today is no different.

To return to Cindy Gladue, she was a legal agent and a legal person according to Cree and Métis law. She made the best decisions she could within the constraints of the power relations she was both within and a part of. What would have happened if there had been recognition for Cindy as a legal agent, legal person, and citizen? And what would have happened if her agency, citizenry, and legal personhood had really shaped and informed the world and relations around her? For Indigenous women and girls, and everyone else, being recognised as legal agents deserving of dignity and safety is essential to rebuilding Indigenous law and Indigenous lawfulness. Legal agency is essential to legal personhood and to law, and vice versa.

I have argued that sexualised and racialised violence against Indigenous women and girls occurs in spaces of lawlessness which is created by undermining Indigenous law resulting in gaps and distortions of Indigenous lawfulness. In light of this, what might the future hold for Indigenous law? In 2018, the University of Victoria launched the first in the world Indigenous law degree programme where after four years, students can obtain a Canadian law degree and an Indigenous law degree (JD/JID). This professional degree programme, along with the UVIC Indigenous Law Research Unit, and the many, many other Indigenous law initiatives across Canada and around the globe, mean that Indigenous law is robustly and critically being rebuilt – substantive law, legal institutions, and processes – and all of this is fundamentally changing the lawscape.

In order for this new lawscape, this explicit multijuridical Canada, to stop the violence against Indigenous women and girls, requires that the enabling sexism and deadly conditions of violence must be recognised up as a serious priority by Indigenous peoples and communities (and obviously, many do), and beyond. The how of this will be worked out over time, and Indigenous lawfulness and safety will be built on the foundation of the JD/JID, and all the other work to restore Indigenous law (Friedland & Napoleon, 2015, 2016; Napoleon & Friedland, 2014).

NOTES

1. Acting Dean and Law Foundation Chair of Indigenous Justice and Governance, Faculty of Law, University of Victoria. I am Cree and a member of the Saulteau First Nation from northeast British Columbia. I am also an adopted member of the House of Luuxhon, Frog Clan, Gitanyow (northern Gitxsan).
2. I lived in Gitxsan territories for several decades and worked in multiple capacities with Gitxsan people in fields of education, justice, economic development, etc.
3. I have expanded on this issue in another paper. See Napoleon (forthcoming).
4. This occurred when I was teaching at the University of Alberta.
5. *Delgamuukw v. British Columbia*, [1997] 3 S.C.R. 1010. The second plaintiff group in *Delgamuukw* was the Wet'suwet'en people.
6. There are a range of legal mechanisms for extending such recognition to non-Gitxsan peoples for political and economic purposes as well as practical arrangements (e.g., marriage to non-Gitxsan).
7. The term 'House' originally derived from the historic Gitxsan longhouses. A longhouse contained extended family lineages and necessarily included people from other kinship groups (Houses) that were married in. In other words, a longhouse population was never the same as a lineage group's membership, that is, House membership.
8. The adaawk is a collective oral history. It is a formal and primary Gitxsan intellectual institution owned by each matrilineal kinship group, the House. It is the adaawk that links each House to its territories and establishes ownership of the land and resources. The

adaawk tell of the origins and migrations of the groups to their current territories, their explorations, the covenants established with the land, and the songs, crests, and names that result from the spiritual connection between people and their land. The adaawk include an architecture, interpretive processes, require public recounting and witnessing, and form an integral part of the structure and operation of Gitxsan governance and law.

9. For different reasons, the Gitxsan also adopt non-Gitxsan, such as the author, into the House system.

10. These societies are diverse belonging to different linguistic groups. The Gitxsan, Tsimshian, and Nisga'a are part of the Tsimshian linguistic group, and some of the Houses share a common early history which is recorded in their respective oral histories. The Wet'suwet'en are part of the Athapaskan linguistic group, the Haisla are part of the Wakashan linguistic group, and the Haida belong to the Haida linguistic group.

11. The last divorce Feast was held during the 1940s. Today, Gitxsan couples use state law for marriage and divorce.

12. Such an adoption requires a formal Feast, a costly undertaking for the host House. Even after such adoptions, there is an ongoing loss of prestige for the couple and sometimes continued public disapproval.

13. Each House has an inventory of names that it owns and that are assigned to its members. When an individual dies, his or her name returns to the House and the House may assign it to another House member. An individual may pass through a number of names before attaining a higher ranking name. When a chief dies, the name is usually immediately passed on to the person in line for the name.

14. There is usually an ongoing internal competition for the chiefs' names in the Houses by the mothers who want to secure the names for their children. Succession of the head chief name can be contested.

15. Susan Marsden was an expert witness on oral histories on behalf of the Gitxsan in the *Delgamuukw* trial.

16. There are examples of gendered and sexual violence in some of the oral histories. See, for example, Cove and MacDonald (1987a, 1987b).

17. This was not an uncommon practice as recounted in some of the oral histories.

18. Indigenous people classified as Indians and registered as status were not allowed to vote in Canadian elections.

19. The report included violence against and experiences of 2SLGBTQQIA or two-spirit, lesbian, gay, bisexual, transgender, queer, questioning, intersex, and asexual.

20. I draw on the work of De Sousa Santos (2013) to approach the problematic nature and issues of human rights in the contested discourse.

REFERENCES

Blatchford, C. (2019, May 24). Christie Blatchford: Her name was not 'native woman' -- a look at the Supreme Court's Cindy Gladue ruling. *National Post*. Retrieved from https://nationalpost.com/opinion/christie-blatchford-her-name-was-not-native-woman-a-look-at-the-supreme-courts-cindy-gladue-ruling?video_autoplay=true

Cove, J. J., & MacDonald, G. F. (Eds.). (1987a). *Tsimshian narratives I: Tricksters, shamans and heroes*. Ottawa: Directorate, Canadian Museum of Civilization.

Cove, J. J., & MacDonald, G. F. (Eds.). (1987b). *Tsimshian narratives II: Trade and warfare*. Ottawa: Directorate, Canadian Museum of Civilization.

De Sousa Santos, B. (2013). *If god were a human rights activist*. Stanford, CA: Stanford University Press.

Friedland, H., & Napoleon, V. (2015). Gathering the threads: Indigenous legal methodology. *Lakehead Law Journal*, *33*, 16–44.

Friedland, H., & Napoleon, V. (2016). An inside job: Engaging with indigenous legal traditions through stories *McGill Law Journal*, *61*(4), 725.

Kiiwetinepinesiik Stark, H., & Starblanket, G. (2018). Towards a relational paradigm – Four points for consideration: Knowledge, gender, land, and modernity. In M. Asch, J. Borrows, & J. Tully (Eds.), *Resurgence and reconciliation* (p. 175). Toronto: University of Toronto Press.

Marsden, S. (2008). Northwest coast Adawx study. In C. Bell & V. Napoleon (Eds.), *First nations cultural heritage and law: Case studies, voices, and perspectives* (p. 121). Vancouver: UBC Press.

Napoleon, V. (2001). Extinction by number: Colonialism made easy. *Canadian Journal of Law and Society*, *16*(1), 113–145.

Napoleon, V. (2002). Raven's garden: A discussion about aboriginal sexual orientation and transgender issues. *Canadian Journal of Law and Society*, *17*(2), 149–171.

Napoleon, V. (2009). Living together: Gitksan legal reasoning as a foundation for consent. In J. Webber & C. McLeod (Eds.), *Challenges of consent: Consent as the foundation of political community in indigenous/non-indigenous contexts* (p. 45). Vancouver: UBC Press.

Napoleon, V. (forthcoming). An imaginary for our sisters: Spirits and indigenous law. In J. Hewitt & R. Moon (Eds.), *Spirituality and Religious Freedom* Toronto: University of Toronto Press. Forthcoming.

Napoleon, V., & Friedland, H. (2014). From roots to renaissance. In M. Dubber (Ed.), *Oxford handbook of criminal law* (pp. 225–247). Oxford: Oxford University Press.

Overstall, R. (2005). Encountering the spirit in the land: 'Property' in a kinship-based legal order. In J. McLaren (Ed.), *Despotic dominion: Property rights in British settler societies* (pp. 22–49). Vancouver: UBC Press.

Rundle, K. (2012). *Forms liberate: Reclaiming the jurisprudence of Lon L Fuller*. Oxford: Hart Publishing.

Rundle, K. (2019). Fuller's relationships. *Archiv für Rechts-und Sozialphilosophie* [*The Journal for Legal and Social Philosophy*], 17–40 (Special edition on 'The Rule of Law and Democracy').

Snyder, E., Napoleon, V., & Borrows, J. (2015). Gendered violence: Resources from Indigenous legal orders. *UBC Law Review*, *48*, (1), 593.

Teillet, J. (2019, May 27). *Globe and Mail*. Retrieved from https://www.theglobeandmail.com/opinion/article-will-there-be-justice-for-cindy-gladue/

Websites

CBC Highway of Tears. Retrieved from https://www.cbc.ca/news/indigenous/jessica-patrick-smithers-highway-of-tears-1.4841697

Ending Violence Association BC. (2005, September 9). *Researched to death: B.C. aboriginal women and violence*. Final Report. Retrieved from http://endingviolence.org/files/uploads/Researched_To_Death_Final_2005.pdf

Highway of Tears. Retrieved from https://www.highwayoftears.ca/

Human Rights Watch. (2013). Those that take us away. Retrieved from https://www.hrw.org/report/2013/02/13/those-who-take-us-away/abusive-policing-and-failures-protection-indigenous-women

Indigenous Law Research Unit. Retrieved from https://www.uvic.ca/law/about/indigenous/indigenouslawresearchunit

National Inquiry into Missing and Murdered Indigenous Women and Girls. (2019a). Executive summary of the reclaiming power and place: The final report of the National Inquiry into Missing and Murdered Indigenous Women and Girls. Retrieved from https://www.mmiwg-ffada.ca/final-report/

National Inquiry into Missing and Murdered Indigenous Women and Girls. (2019b). Reclaiming power and place: The final report of the National Inquiry into Missing and Murdered Indigenous Women and Girls. Retrieved from https://www.mmiwg-ffada.ca/final-report/

Truth and Reconciliation Commission of Canada. Retrieved from https://nctr.ca/assets/reports

Court Cases

Delgamuukw v. *British Columbia*, [1997] 3 S.C.R. 1010.

Legislation

Indian Act, R.S.C. 1985, c. 1-5.

Indian Act, 1876, s. 61. See Indian and Northern Affairs Canada, Chapter 18: An act to amend and consolidate the laws respecting Indians. April 12, 1876. Retrieved from http://www.ainc-inac.gc.ca/ai/arp/ls/pubs/1876c18/1876c18-eng.asp

CHAPTER 3

FOUCAULT'S PERHAPS: MADNESS, SUFFERING AND THE INTERRUPTION OF LEGAL PERSONALITY IN FOUCAULT, SUPIOT AND HEGEL

Johan van der Walt

ABSTRACT

In his work Homo Juridicus, *Alain Supiot considers the construction of legal personality by force and virtue of law as a precondition for human liberty. Michel Foucault views this same construction of legal personality – the construction of the subject through strategies of power, he calls it – as a 'construction' of liberty that is considerably less free than it is made out to be by the Enlightenment law reform projects proposed by Cesare Beccaria and other prominent eighteenth century law reformers. Foucault's scepticism vis-á-vis Beccaria and others evidently also implies a critical stance vis-á-vis contemporary humanist understandings of law such as Supiot's. This chapter will endeavour to explain what is at stake in the difference between these very different conceptions of legal personality by relating it to the problematics of subjectivity that came to the fore in the thinking of Hegel and the German Idealists.*

Keywords: Foucault; Supiot; Hegel; *homo juridicus*; legal person; theory of subjectivity; theory of the subject

Interrupting the Legal Person
Studies in Law, Politics, and Society, Volume 87A, 33–48

Published under exclusive licence by Emerald Publishing Limited
ISSN: 1059-4337/doi:10.1108/S1059-433720220000087A003

1. INTRODUCTION

According to Alain Supiot, human life is conditioned by two births. The first birth concerns the commencement of physical or biological human life, but this birth, claims Supiot, does not yet bring into existence a complete human being. Complete human existence only begins after the second birth – the birth into law that starts with the subjection of the physical and natural body of the human individual to the laws of language. The infant – the one without language – becomes human by acquiring language, and language is acquired through subjection to the laws of the language of the mother. The mother, claims Supiot, is therefore the first and most formidable legislator that compels the infant to replace or supplement its exclusively biological existence for the sake of entering human existence (Supiot, 2005, pp. 7–8).

The acquisition of language is but the first step of the entry into the law-conditioned existence that completes the human being. According to Supiot, the human being becomes a person, and thus a human being in the full sense of the word, through the recognition and safeguarding of the person that the law affords every human individual. In other words, the human individual becomes fully human by virtue of legal rules and enforceable interdicts that recognise and safeguard the person. For Supiot, the human person is therefore essentially a *legal person*, an instantiation of *homo juridicus*. Law conditions and completes the human status of the human individual.

Supiot's legal anthropology is unhistorical. He does not ask questions about the epochal development of law that traversed many phases before something like a general – let alone 'universal' – recognition of legal personality became a plausible notion, albeit a plausible notion burdened by many inconsistencies and contradictions. The awareness that all major systems of law have for millennia only recognised the human status of some human beings and for all practical purposes continue to do so today (see Gündoğdu, 2015) does not seem to bother Supiot's conception of the human person as essentially an instance of *homo juridicus*.

Michel Foucault proposes a very different view of *homo juridicus*. Foucault is well known for unmasking the humanist notion of 'the human' as a contingent historical construction. Showing up the historical contingency of all humanistic conceptions of human existence is the centre-piece of his scholarly legacy. He not only pointed out the 'recentness' of the claim that law recognises the human person as normatively entitled to universally valid standards of legal protection (*on peut être sûr que l'homme [européen] … est une invention récente* – Foucault, 1966, p. 398). He also questioned the substance of this claim fundamentally, hence his dismissal of this claim with a supercilious 'perhaps'. The legal reforms of the eighteenth century were widely considered to render the law more human, observed Foucault. Perhaps they also did that, he conceded in passing. But their real aim, he stressed, was very definitely to pursue a new strategy. Here is the key statement from *Surveiller et punir* at issue here:

> The attenuation of the severity of punishment in the course of the last centuries is a phenomenon that is well known among historians of law. But it has for a long time predominantly been taken as a quantitative phenomenon: 'less cruelty, less suffering, more moderation, more

> respect, more humanity'. In fact, these modifications are accompanied by a shift in the very goal of the penal process. Diminishing of its intensity? Perhaps [*Peut-être*]. Change of goal, certainly [*à coup sûr*]. (Foucault, 1975, pp. 23–24, my translation)

This chapter engages with the dismissive 'perhaps' that Foucault inserted into this passage (*pp* for 'perhaps passage' from now on). It is important to note the tenor and status of this brief *perhaps*, this *peut-être* that also in the French text stands isolated between sentences. It comes across as a brief interjection to which Foucault paid no or little attention. This *perhaps*, wontedly or not, is nevertheless a pivotal point on which a deep enigma in Foucault's can be argued to turn. It is also the critical point where Foucault's and Supiot's very different readings of *homo juridicus* take leave of one another. But they take leave of one another, I shall argue, only to sustain one another. Supiot and Foucault evidently put forward two contradicting conceptions of *homo juridicus*. One should nevertheless not 'choose' between them, because choosing the one *homo juridicus* at the expense of the other necessarily destroys the precondition that sustains the 'chosen' one.

Taken together, Foucault's and Supiot's respective conceptions of the legal conditions of personhood underline the irreducible two-sidedness of the legal person and the split on which this two-sidedness pivots. This, then, is the angle that this chapter takes on the 'interruption of legal personality' interrogated by the chapters in this volume. The 'interruption of the legal person', I shall argue, concerns the constitutive split between two *homines juridici* that precariously parade as one *homo juridicus*. The interminable precariousness of this parade, I shall also argue, is the function of the doubled or twofold contingency that results from its double-sidedness. I shall explain this twofold contingency of *homo juridicus* with recourse to the 'perhaps' in *pp* in four sections. Section 2 begins by construing this perhaps as a 'double-sided perhaps'. Section 3 turns to a comparison of Supiot's and Foucault's respective conceptions of *homo juridicus* for purposes of marking the coordinates of an interrupted legal person. Section 4 ties the 'interruption of the legal person' to the 'double-sided perhaps' expounded in Section 2. Section 5 relates the 'interruption of the legal person' to the interruption of subjectivity already contemplated by Hegel. Section 6 concludes the argument by underlining the inevitability of the interruption of the legal person and the subject, and stresses the need to sustain both *homines juridici* that step out of this interruption, however out of step they are destined to remain. Their parade is not a charade. It is nothing less than the constitutive concern of the politics of personhood.

2. FOUCAULT'S DOUBLE-SIDED PERHAPS

The supercilious character of the 'perhaps' in *pp* can hardly be missed. It quite evidently communicates Foucault's view that it is not even necessary to interrogate the Enlightenment ideals of law and universal human rights further. One would nevertheless miss something significant about *pp* were one to reduce it to the element of superciliousness that may well be part of it. One would miss the way in which the 'perhaps' in *pp* affects and even unsettles the 'certainly' or 'sûr' that follows in its wake. And once one realises that the 'perhaps' in *pp* unsettles and even undoes the 'certainly' that follows so short on its heels, one also begins to realise that the 'perhaps' in *pp* actually alerts one to the much deeper problematic that comes to the fore in Foucault's whole oeuvre. That is why we will take this 'perhaps' as much more than a supercilious dismissal of the humanist and Enlightenment narrative of eighteenth century law reforms. We shall construe it as a critical joint on Foucault's whole oeuvre hinges.

The counter-narrative that Foucault invoked in response to the humanist narratives of Enlightenment legal and social theorists is well known. Instead of – or at least in addition to – making the law more human, these narratives gave birth to an incessantly surveilled person (see Foucault, 1975, pp. 201–208) that is constantly measured against the yardstick of the 'healthy human being' produced by the social or human sciences (see Foucault, 1966, especially pp. 355–398). This constant surveillance and measurement of the human person *created* the human person, it did not impose itself on a person 'already there'. It effectively fashioned the healthy human being for purposes of rendering stable and secure a society that is ultimately concerned with nothing but rendering itself stable and secure. To put this all in the nutshell of *pp*: The humanist narratives of eighteenth century law reforms have *perhaps* (*peut-être*) given rise to more humane law, but it *certainly* (*sûr*) also promoted a system of surveillance and normalising practices that belie the ideals of the freedom and dignity of the person.

One might think at first glance that the 'perhaps' in *pp* only conditions the phrases that precede it. One may think that the 'perhaps' only casts doubt on the humanist narrative invoked in the first half of the passage, and not on that which follows. It does not affect the '*sûr*' inserted into the last line of the passage. The inevitable double-sidedness of the 'perhaps' in the passage must nevertheless not be ignored. If the Enlightenment ideals *perhaps* gave rise to legal systems that promoted legal dignity and freedom, it also could only *perhaps* have given rise to systems of de-humanising and liberty-depriving surveillance and normalisation. The effect of the 'perhaps' cannot be restricted to only one side of the set of options of concern. It cuts both ways. If a possible state of affairs is subject to a 'perhaps', its opposite is logically subject to the same 'perhaps'. One must therefore conclude that Foucault's counter-narrative about the normalisation that fashions the human subject is as much subject to the perhaps to which he expressly subjected the humanist narrative in the first part of the passage.

Subjecting Foucault's counter-narrative to the counter-side of the 'perhaps' that he attached to the humanist narrative about eighteenth century law reforms undoubtedly unsettles this counter-narrative. But it also does something else. By unsettling his counter-narrative, the 'perhaps' creates an opening in Foucault's own thinking for the very thought that motivates his counter-narrative, but does not sit well with it. Foucault's genealogical enterprise is not exactly a gay science. It is not a merry explication of the wondrous ways of power in the world and of the neat and comfortable space power creates for human existence. It contemplates, at least in its wings, a person that somehow resists power or experience resistance to it, as I shall show presently. It is fair to suppose that his whole scholarly engagement is ultimately motivated by a regard for this person who escapes from – however narrowly – the relentless reach of his genealogical method. This person, however, cannot exist outside the reach of his genealogies unless their reach is subject to a limit. It should be clear from what we have said thus far that Foucault's whole genealogical method prevents him from invoking something like 'true human nature' that experiences itself constrained, betrayed, or alienated by current constructions of humanity and current conceptions of the dignity and freedom of the person. To put it in terms that are reminiscent of a famous phrase of Jacques Derrida (1967): There is *no person* outside the constructions of personality, let alone a 'true person' (See p. 227, 'There is nothing outside the text' – *il n'y a pas de hors-texte*). Foucault (2002) put it like this in a key passage from the lecture 'Truth and Juridical Forms':

> What I intend to show in these lectures is how, in actual fact, the political and economic conditions of existence are not a veil or an obstacle for the subject of knowledge but the means by which subjects of knowledge are formed, and hence are truth relations. There cannot be particular types of subjects of knowledge, orders of truth, or domains of knowledge except on the basis of the political conditions that are the very ground on which the subject, the domains of knowledge, and the relations of truth are formed. (p. 15)

It is on the basis of this same insight or claim that Foucault observed later in this same lecture, contra Marx, that the capitalist economy does not effect an alienation of labour or work (considered by Marx the noble essence of man), but, much more fundamentally, constructs the human individual as a being that works and has to work (Foucault, 2002, p. 86). The question that this passage and the later statement contra Marx raise is this: what, after all, can this talk about un-dignifying and liberty-depriving normalisations of the person or subject be about if the person is *nothing but* the function of normalising practices? How can an entirely constructed and normalised individual be at variance with itself? How can it possess a residue of unconstructed 'authentic' selfhood that suffers from this construction and normalisation? If a worker has been exhaustively constructed and normalised as a worker, how can he or she still experience the fate of being a worker as a deprivation of liberty and dignity? The experience of such deprivation necessarily depends on some residue of unconstructed personality that is not reconciled with just being 'a worker'.

Did Foucault ever acknowledge the possibility of such a residue of unconstructed and non-normalised personhood? He did. He evidently found evidence of such an interruption in a certain madness beyond madness, a *déraison* beyond the normalising pathologies constructed by the human sciences, and in an *idiocy* that resists its own nothingness. He asks with regard to Goya's idiot:

> The idiot who cries and contorts his shoulder in order to escape from the nothingness that imprisons him [*au néant qui l'imprisonne*], is he the birth of the first human and its first step towards freedom, or the final contraction of the last one dying? (Foucault, 1972, p. 551, my translation)

Is this madness or idiocy the interruption that affords Foucault the slender chance – the most precarious 'perhaps' – of embarking on the thinking of an impossible outside? (see Foucault, 1986). Foucault ultimately leaves this dramatic question unanswered, and thus effectively underlines the uncertainty of any escape from the strategies of power that he discerns in insanity, especially the insanity of the mad poet (Foucault, 1972, pp. 555–557). But, the singular existence of the exponentially-raised derangement – the derangement beyond derangement – of the mad poet did signal for Foucault a shadowy figure that somehow exists independently of all clinical diagnoses that pretend to give measurable or calculable form to it. This is the undeniable signal sent in the last chapters of *Histoire de la folie*. And this shadowy existence also makes fleeting appearances in *Surveiller et punir* where the convicted and punished criminal takes the place of the mad poet in *Histoire de la folie*. Consider the following two passages:

> Mably has formulated the principle once and for all: 'That punishment, if I can speak like this, strikes the soul rather than the body'. This is an important moment. The old partners of the punitive pageant, body and blood, vacate the scene. A new personage appears on stage, masked. This the end of a certain tragedy; and a comedy commences with the silhouettes of shadows, voices without faces and untouchable entities. The apparatus of justice now has to bite on this reality without body. (Foucault, 1975, p. 24, my translation)

> In the name of crimes and delicts, one indeed always judges objects defined by the Code, but one also judges – in the same breath – passions, instincts, anomalies, weaknesses, maladjustments, environmental or hereditary effects. One punishes aggressions, but through them aggressive inclinations. One punishes rape, but also the perversions that drive it; one punishes murders, but also the impulses and desires that lead to them. They will say: it is not them – the criminals and their passions – who are judged. If one invokes them, it is only to explain the facts that are to be judged, and to determine to what extent the will of subject is implicated in the crime. This response is inadequate, because it is them, the shadows behind these elements of the criminal case, who are well and truly judged and punished. (Foucault, 1975, p. 25, my translation)

These passages make clear that there is some sort of separation thinkable or perceivable between the construction of the criminal personality and the one that suffers from the consequences of this construction. They invoke a separation that allows the constructed subject to suffer from the process and result of construction. Foucault's genealogies (notwithstanding his denials) ultimately come across, then, as a methodological procedure that allows him to step into the vicinity of something or someone to which or whom the methodological procedure itself refuses to grant independent existence.

Of concern here would appear to be an interruption of construction, an interruption of the construction of criminal personality and an interruption of the legal person as such. And the interruption to which Foucault appears to testify is not only an interruption of Supiot's humanist legal person, the subject figure to whom the law gives adequate personality by affording it a second birth. It is nothing less than an interruption of Foucault's own anti-humanist genealogies of subjectivity. Nothing less than a gap in Foucault's oeuvre – and a self-interruption of this oeuvre – becomes evident when Foucault invokes the shadowy figure that suffers from the genesis of subjectivity.

3. FOUCAULT, SUPIOT AND THE LEGAL PERSON – A TALE OF TWO *HOMINES JURIDICI*

The tension that existed between Derrida and Foucault regarding the latter's invocation of a madness beyond clinical mental illness should not be denied or underestimated (for a probing discussion, see Jonas, 2015). However, that tension may well have been the result of the way in which the two thinkers endeavoured to establish at least some degree of uniqueness and specificity of position within a common space that they all too clearly shared, a common space that allowed them both to consider madness the signal of an 'outside' that cannot be assimilated by law or the strategies of power, however ubiquitous and without 'outside' the empires of law and power appear to be. For both Foucault and Derrida, the road to the 'real man' would seem to pass through the mad man, to use Foucault's (1972) expression in this regard – *de l'homme à l'homme vrai le chemin passe par l'homme fou* (p. 544). Seen from this perspective, the following comment of Alain Supiot on Derrida's notion of a 'mad justice' (*justice fou*) may well be a sign of how Supiot might assess Foucault's concern with madness:

> This (indeed mad) definition of justice, connected to the solitary subjectivity of everyone and aimed at the deconstruction of law, is the philosophical manifestation of the disqualification of social justice by ultra-liberals, who consider justice a sentiment that is incapable of founding a system of law worthy of the name. (Supiot, 2010, p. 48, my translation)

Considering this response to Derrida, one may well assume that Supiot would be disinclined to discern the utopian potential in the phenomenon of madness that Foucault explores in the last chapters of *Histoire de la Folie*. From Supiot's perspective (see Supiot 2015, pp. 177–178), Foucault's whole preoccupation with governmentality, bio-power, normalisation and surveillance evidently comes across as part and parcel of a libertarian and neoliberal-friendly obsession with deregulation (as indeed also suggested forcefully by Audier, 2015, pp. 509–512, 521–527), notwithstanding his own frequent use of terminology that can hardly be distinguished from Foucault's, as will be observed presently. His express association of both Derrida and Foucault with 'that old undertaking … to make law "wither away"' speaks volumes in this regard (see Supiot, 2005, pp. 23–24, fn. 3). Supiot (2005), on the contrary, considers subjection to law the 'second birth of the person' (pp. 7–8, 221) without which the person never attains to personhood. He stresses in this regard 'the anthropological function of human laws' and the need to recognise 'the role of law in constructing individual and collective identities' (Supiot, 2005, p. 128). He views proper regulation as part and parcel of a legal system of interdicts (*interdits*) with which humans say to one another (say among themselves – *inter-dire*) how the human being is to be treated (Supiot, 2005, pp. 30, 184). Of concern for Supiot is the system of interdicts that prevents everyone from dealing with anyone else in a way that violates, denies or disrespects the dignity of the legal person. The law is for him the system of interdicts that prevents everyone from reducing the human being to mere matter. This reduction was the essence of the big totalitarian ideological movements of the twentieth century and it is also the essence of the total market thinking of our time. According to Supiot, the ultra-liberal market ideology of our time also turns on a materialist reduction of humanity to matter and quantifiable data. It is remarkable, however, how frequently he describes this materialist reduction in terms that are palpably and sometimes expressly Foucauldian (see Supiot, 2005, pp. 187–189, 210–212, 228, 225; 2010, pp. 59–74, 2015, p. 135).

One must therefore note the striking resonance between Supiot's legal anthropology and Foucault's discourse-analytical genealogies, notwithstanding their 'opposite trajectories' and the opposite trajectories of being human that become evident through them. This resonance has not received significant attention in literature on either Supiot or Foucault (for some unthematised links between them, or at least invocations of both with regard to the same problematic, see Bartl et al., 2019; Diaz-Bone, 2015; Dujarier, 2010; Haroche, 2010). However, notwithstanding the vociferous anti-humanist protestations characteristic of Foucault's genealogies and the evidently humanist purport of Supiot's legal anthropology, both ultimately invoke the idea of 'something human' that exists beyond normalisation, standardisation or quantification. The difference between them concerns the respective roles that they attribute to the law as regards this unquantifiable element of humanity. For Supiot, the law safeguards the human and humanity against quantification. For Foucault, the law is the essential mechanism of quantification. Supiot's position is consistent. Foucault's is not. As we saw, he holds on to his narrative of exhaustive governmental construction and normalisation while also holding on to a residue of unconstructed and non-normalised humanity. Can these contradictory sides of his thinking be reconciled? It can, I shall now argue, when one extrapolates the *perhaps* that he slipped into *pp* and considers it the crucial joint that holds his whole oeuvre together.

4. THE DOUBLE-SIDED 'PERHAPS' IN THE INTERRUPTION OF THE LEGAL PERSON

It seems possible to simply infer from the arguments above that the interruption of legal personality concerns the gap in the 'subject' that becomes evident in Supiot's and Foucault's very different assessments of legal personality. For the former, legal personality is the very condition for and completion of human dignity and liberty; for the latter, it is the frustration of a human dignity and liberty that persist in the shadows of legal personality, that is, a dignity and liberty that exist in the shadows of the frustrating termination that endows it with positive existence. This view of the interruption of the legal person – consisting of nothing but an arbitrary juxtaposing of two theories that contradict one another – remains groundless. More argument is required to give it cogency. In this section of this chapter, I endeavour to find this cogency in the way this interruption of the legal person also features inside Foucault's oeuvre. Of specific concern will be the tension or contradiction in his work highlighted above. It is crucial not to view this contradiction or tension as a negligent contradiction that clouds his work with inconsistency. It should be viewed instead as a constituent paradox of which all the elements – both sides of it, so to speak – are fully dependent on one another. I shall illuminate this paradox now by connecting the two sides of Foucault's thought to the double-sided 'perhaps' that he inserted into *pp*.

We saw that Foucault juxtaposes two narratives about personhood in *pp*, the Enlightenment or humanist narrative that he seems to dismiss with a floating 'perhaps', and the counter-narrative of governmental construction and normalisation that he presents as a certainty. I have already shown above that Foucault's perhaps cuts both ways. If Bentham's and Beccaria's (and by implication Supiot's) humanist narratives are affected by it, so is Foucault's own project. I shall now argue that Foucault's own project is not only affected by this double-sided perhaps, it is also crucially dependent on it. The double-side perhaps is the indispensable joint that holds the apparently contradictory sides of his theory of personhood together. It explains why the shadowy figure in the margin of his counter-narrative of governmental construction and normalisation does not contradict this counter-narrative, but necessarily results from it. It results from it because of the way in which the counter-narrative itself remains subject to an irreducible perhaps. The shadowy figure in the margin of Foucault's counter-narrative is a surprising side-effect of a double-sided 'perhaps'. It is this double-sided 'perhaps' that furnishes his entire methodological procedure – the procedure that generally considers legal personality a result of normalisation and disciplinary subject-formation – with a boundary that halts its sweeping effect. It opens up a narrow space – indeed a margin – within which can appear the shadowy figure that is not just an effect of normalisation, but also the signal of an independent existence, the signal of an existence that is independent enough from normalisation to suffer from it.

Why? Why does the 'double-sided perhaps' establish a margin within the narrow space of which the shadowy figure invoked in the second and third passages from *Surveiller et Punir* quoted above remains free to dwell? We saw from these passages that the subject constructed by the scene of judgement, conviction and punishment that the system of penal law stages is nevertheless not exhaustively constructed by this scene. There remains a shadowy rest of unconstructed personhood – or of something or someone – that is not fully captured by the penal system, a rest that remains free or independent enough from this system to suffer from it. The 'suffering' that Foucault ascribes to this 'shadowy rest' is the tell-tale sign that this 'rest' is not exhaustively assimilated by the stage of criminal law. Now, what exactly is the connection between the 'double-sided perhaps' and the shadowy rest of untouched freedom that the legal system cannot capture or accommodate? This question leads one directly to the last syllogism of the argument that I am unpacking here. It goes like this: if Foucault's 'perhaps' affords the Enlightenment narrative of legal personhood some chance of occasional and/or partial 'success' (as showed above), that partial or occasional success must be considered potential proof of the partial and occasional failure of Foucault's own genealogical method. Strictly speaking, Foucault's method implies a whole sale dismissal of the Enlightenment narrative of personhood. The Enlightenment narrative would be completely delusionary if Foucault's genealogical method were fully correct. But, the 'perhaps' in *pp* expressly qualifies this whole sale dismissal (irrespective of whether it does so wontedly or unwontedly) and thus limits the reach of the genealogical method; hence the possibility or plausibility of invoking a shadowy figure beyond the reach of the genealogical method, a figure that narrowly sidesteps the exhaustive construction and normalisation that a complete genealogical method would ascribe to it, him.

The shadowy figure in the margin of Foucault's genealogical method is of course not the autonomous self – endowed with inviolable dignity, integrity, etc. –

that the Enlightenment narrative of personality contemplates. The shadowy figure beyond construction and normalisation that Foucault contemplates is much more akin to the romantic hero (or anti-hero) that resists construction and normalisation to the point of sheer derangement and self-destruction. This, in any case, is what the line of thinking pursued towards the end of *Histoire de la folie* suggests, and we will return to this 'romantic' element in Foucault's thinking, below. The important point to note here, however, is this: the narrow chance of success that Foucault grants the Enlightenment narrative of autonomous personhood is also crucial for the plausibility of the ghostly romantic hero that he himself seeks to salvage from the relentless sweep of his own genealogical method. Or vice versa! The reversal of the argument is even more important from the perspective of the Enlightenment narrative: the remainder of the ghostly romantic hero in the margins of Foucault's genealogical method constitutes a crucial point of departure for any argument that seeks to limit the sweep of Foucault's genealogical method for the sake of saving from it the possibility of a person who is not just constructed and normalised by the law, but one to whom the law also grants autonomy, dignity and integrity.

It should be clear now why the 'perhaps' in *pp* has received all the attention that it has received above, and why the double-sidedness of this perhaps must be duly recognised. The double-sidedness of this 'perhaps' not only affords the Enlightenment narrative of personhood a chance by subjecting the genealogical method to a limit, it also affords plausibility to Foucault's contemplation of the shadowy remains of an authentic romantic hero that remains invisible to the panoptic factories of modern subjectivity. His own thinking of the 'outside' is fundamentally dependent on the imposition of a limit on his genealogical method. That is why one can also insist here that the significance attributed to the 'perhaps' above, is not just the outcome of an artful exegesis of passage taken randomly from *Surveiller et Punir*. The double-sided 'perhaps' that is of concern here happens to go to the heart of Foucault's project. It is in a fundamental sense *Foucault's perhaps*, not just the randomly magnified 'perhaps' taken from a passage into which he may have slipped it without much thought, and not without an element of rhetorical superciliousness. It was stressed from the beginning of this chapter that Foucault may well have slipped that 'perhaps' into *pp* without giving much thought to it. That does not matter. In fact, the passage as such need not be taken that seriously. Now that it has done its work, it can be discarded. It is not 'proof' of anything. I have only relied on it because the choice of words and phrasing exercised in it happens to facilitate an instructive explanation of a pivotal joint in Foucault's thinking. This pivotal joint in his thinking, I shall now show, is also not just some peculiar feature of his thinking that happens to be key to *his* genealogical project. It has been coming a long way. It pertains to the way European philosophers have been thinking at least since Kant, Fichte, Schelling and Hegel.

5. THE INTERRUPTION OF THE PERSON IN GERMAN IDEALISM

Giorgio Agamben's essay 'What is an apparatus?' takes us to the heart of the apparent link between Foucault's thought and German Idealism. Agamben points out that the French word for 'apparatus', *dispositif*, commenced to feature increasingly in Foucault's texts in the mid-1970s. Before this time, the word 'positivity' – *positivité* in French – was the more current expression in Foucault's texts for that which he later commenced to call '*dispositif*'. 'Positivity' is a key term in the philosophy of Hegel, and Foucault must have picked up through the work of Jean Hyppolite, claims Agamben, given the centrality of this term in Hyppolite's influential *Introduction à la philosophie de l'histoire de Hegel*, and considering the importance of Hyppolite's mentorship on the young Foucault (Agamben, 2009, pp. 1–8).

In his early essay *Die positivität der christliche Religion*, Hegel drew a distinction between natural and positive religions that became a crucial element of the dialectic thinking that he developed in his later works. Natural religion, argued the young Hegel, allows for the expression of a completely spontaneous and immediate relation of human reason with the divine, whereas positive religion casts the relation between human reason and the divine in positivised forms or moulds such as clearly articulated articles of faith and ethical rules. The 'positivity of the Christian religion' concerned its suspension of all spontaneous and immediate relationships with God and their replacement with positivised articles of the Christian faith and the positive ethical rules concomitant to them. A positive set of beliefs, ethical commands and proscriptions would henceforth constitute the Christian community's – and the Christian individual's – only connection with the divine or sacred. It was the task of philosophy, argued the young Hegel, to overcome this 'positivisation' of the Christian's relation with the divine. He explained this positivisation in terms of an 'objectification' of 'subjectivity'. It was the task of philosophy to undo the objectivisation of the self's relation to the divine, by reinfusing it with the subjectivity (spontaneous expression) that it had lost. Of concern in this objectification of subjectivity, Hyppolite pointed out in his work on Hegel's philosophy of history, is the same tension between subjective reason, and the objective formulations or formats through which reason realises itself (takes positive form) in the different phases of its history. Hippolyte referred to these objective articulations of reason in the course of its historical development as the '*historical element*' of reason (see Agamben, 2009, p. 5).

Anyone with some understanding of Hegel's mature metaphysical system can easily see how its key terms – the dialectic between subjective and objective spirit through which spirit overcomes its own divisions and objectifications in the course of history so as to become Absolute Spirit at the end of history – derive from the concepts of subjectivity and positivity that he developed in his early work on natural and positive religion. Now, it is also very well known that Foucault expressly considered his own work an endeavour to break away from Hegel's dialectic metaphysics of history (see Foucault, 2002, pp. 241, 246). It nevertheless remains a good question whether this endeavour succeeded, as he himself acknowledged (see Foucault, 1971, pp. 74–75, as well as the probing discussions in Allen, 1998; Butler, 1999, pp. 217–231; Gutting, 2010; Jameson, 2009, pp. 51–52, 120–123; Künzel, 1985; Muldoon, 2014; Sembou, 2015).

During the same time and even some years before the word 'apparatus' (*dispositif*) began to replace the word positivity (*positivité*) in the work of Foucault, according to Agamben, several German scholars were also highlighting the enduring significance of these early distinctions between subjectivity and positivity (or objectivisation) for Hegel's later work (see, for instance, Rohrmoser, 1961 and Lypp, 1978). These scholars, to whom Agamben surprisingly does not refer (he usually refers to everything), emphasised the central role that the terms *Subjektivität* and *Verdinglichung* – subjectivity and reification – played in Hegel's early works, and how it came to determine key elements of the dialectic philosophy of his later work.

It took a while before Hegel 's insight into the 'positivity' of the Christian religion actually moved him to discard religion and turn to philosophy in his search for a reconciliation between subject and object and the overcoming of the hard opposition between spontaneous selfhood and the ever-hardening positivity of life in modern societies. He basically persisted throughout his Bern–Frankfurt period with the idea that the religious subjectivity embodied in Christian love offers the only way out of the fragmented division of subject and object and the resulting positvisation or reification of social relations in the modern age. It is only during his Jena years and notably in his essay on the difference between Schelling's and Fichte's philosophical systems – commonly known as the *Differenzschrift* (see Hegel, 1970a) – that philosophy displaced religion and took over from it the task of reconciling the subject and the object so as to reinfuse reified objective reality with the subjectivity that it lost as a result of the split between the subject and the object (the withdrawal of the subject from the object that historically conditioned the Modern Age, according to Hegel). It is in the *Differenzschrift* that Hegel articulated his famous statement on the need for philosophy that arises when life has become too weak to overcome its own divisions (see Hegel, 1970a, p. 22). Hegel continued to resort to this philosophical reconciliation of the subject and the object in the years after 1801 (when the *Differenzschrift* was published) and it became the cornerstone of his later works, most notably the *Phänomenologie des Geistes* published in 1807. This philosophical reconciliation never (except perhaps for a section in the *Grundlinien der Philosophie des Rechts* – see Van der Walt, 2019, pp. 135–167) claimed to actually mend the subject–object split and to eradicate the reification of the object. On the contrary, it proposed a 'philosophical' acceptance (in the way one says someone was 'philosophical' about a loss) of the split between the subject and the inevitability of reification in the modern world. In other words, Hegel's mature philosophy pivoted on the insight that subjectivity and reification (or positivity) necessarily go together. The subject becomes the subject by withdrawing from the object and this withdrawal necessarily leaves the object reified (devoid of subjectivity). A key passage in the *Phänomenologie des Geistes* underlines this torn status (*Zerrisenheit*) of 'spiritual existence'. Ultimately at stake in this inseparability of subjectivity and reification is the inseparability of the life and death of the subject (see Hegel, 1970c, p. 36). The crucial point to take from this passage, is this: The human person belongs inextricably to both worlds, the world of subjective freedom or autonomy and the world of reified objectivity. As a legal person in particular, the autonomous self also belongs to the institutional positivity of the law and must reconcile itself with the fact that the law protects subjective autonomy, but also frustrates it to the core. Hence, also the elegiac statement in the introduction to the *Grundlinien der Philosophie des Rechts* that the consolidation of the modern state and the rule of law, besides being the historical and positive realisation of liberty, is also the sign of life that has grown old and incapable of renewing itself (Hegel, 1970b, p. 28).

This is admittedly a very simplified outline of one of the most complex issues in Hegel's work, an issue with regard to which he also took different positions over the years, and sometimes also different positions in the same work. The *Grundlinien der Philosophie des Rechts* can certainly be said to contain passages that mend or erase the torn state of subjectivity which the *Differenzschrift*, *Phänomenologie* and even its own preface underline. Space constraints prohibit deeper engagement with this complex Hegelian background here (see Van der Walt, 2019 for a more extensive discussion), but at least one more elucidation is necessary before we move on to conclude these reflections. Hegel's shifting and even contradictory conceptions of the relation between spontaneous selfhood or freedom, on the one hand, and alienated or alienating social and natural environments, on the other, can be traced to the different influences that the other members of the German Idealist movement had on his thinking. The concern with a complete reconciliation between subject and object and the restoration of the unity and totality of existence that is more typical of his early works was predominantly influenced by the romantic pantheism of Schelling. The regard for the inevitably split condition of modern existence and the inevitable divide between the subject and object that is more typical of his later work was predominantly influenced by the Enlightenment concern with subjective autonomy as the moral withdrawal from and overcoming of objective nature that is central to the work of Kant and Fichte (see Rohrmoser, 1961, pp. 95–96). The insight into this split condition of modern life on which the shift from Schelling to Kant and Fichte pivoted was also fundamentally informed by his reading of the British political economists. It is through the works of James Steuart, David Ricardo and Adam Smith (and later also the French economist Jean-Babtiste Say) that Hegel came to understand the irredeemably alienated and split condition of modern life (see Riedel, 1975, pp. 260–261; Ritter, 2003, p. 218). This tension between Romantic concerns with unity and pantheistic immersion, and Enlightenment concerns with autonomous selfhood continues to reverberate in the tensions between Foucault's and Supiot's respective conceptions of *homo juridicus*. In fact, it goes to the heart of the interruption of the legal person, I shall now argue in conclusion.

6. *HOMINES JURIDICI*

The first question that one should ask in view of the problematic of personhood in the thinking of the German Idealists concerns the Hegelian or post-Hegelian status of Foucault's concern with personhood and selfhood. Does Foucault's constellation of a constructed and normalised subject (replete with *positivity* and largely reduced to an *apparatus* of governance) and the shadowy rest of autonomy and liberty (that dwells in the margin of this normalised and constructed subjectivity) break with the German Idealist and especially Hegelian articulation of this problematic, or is it yet another configuration of this idealist articulation of personhood? The second question depends on the outcome of the first. If a case can be made that Foucault broke decisively with the German Idealist problematic, there is no second question. If not, if one accepts that Foucault does not effectively break away from the Hegelian position on selfhood, but just rearticulates it, the second question is whether Foucault is leaning to the romantic or the Enlightenment side of Hegel's position. Is Foucault (quite paradoxically) closer to Schelling, or is he closer to Kant and Fichte? Both the shadowy figure that dwells on the outside of the apparatus of the person constructed by penal law and the exponentially raised madness of the poet that dwells on the outside of the clinic seem to allude to a romantic hero (or anti-hero) that has little in common with the moral autonomy of the subject that Kant and Fichte contemplated. This is nevertheless just a preliminary observation. Neither of these questions can be answered here. They can only be posed for purposes of further reflection.

However, what can be observed with confidence in view of all the reflections above is this: there is enough evidence of a firm perception in the history of modern philosophy and contemporary social and legal theory that human selfhood is burdened by two opposite and mutually contradicting existential concerns, a concern with the construction of a stable institutional and legal environment that guarantees the moral autonomy envisaged by the Enlightenment narrative of personhood, on the one hand, and a concern with a romantic existential freedom that experiences the positivity of all institutional and legal arrangements as reifications of the human being's spontaneous and primordial connectedness with its social and natural environment. This observation (echoes of which are also evident in Esposito, 2012) appears to go to the heart of the fundamentally different understandings of law and legal personality that come to the work in the work of Michel Foucault and Alain Supiot outlined above.

The crucial point stressed in the juxta-positioning of Supiot's and Foucault's work above concerns the precariousness and uncertainty of both their respective concerns with the legal protection and construction of personhood. The double-sided perhaps extracted from *pp* tells us that neither of their concerns with the person has the luxury of stability and certainty. The law that guarantees personal autonomy in terms of the Enlightenment narrative of moral autonomy remains fragile because of the way it frustrates the existential concern with a primordial and spontaneous unity with the world. The existential concern with an intimate unity with the world that allows for and somehow does not ruin or constrain the spontaneity of selfhood is even more precarious. In fact, the Modern Age has largely subjected this concern to the concern with moral autonomy. Modernity has largely reduced the concern with the spontaneous self to a fictional or poetic concern. It has largely become the concern of the mad poet, as Foucault understood all too well. And whenever this concern with a spontaneous unity between the self and its world became frustrated with the constraints of this poetic reduction or reduction to poetry, whenever it commenced to contemplate non-fictional revivals of a communal politics capable of restoring a primordial bond between the self and its social environment that is untarnished by institutional and normalising representations of the self (note the current world-wide wave of populist resistances to representative and representational democracy), it would inevitably turn into an anti-modern concern with an ancient paradise lost.

The point is nevertheless not to choose between these two precarious narratives and these two sides of the *perhaps*. Neither of them will yield to complete suppression or eradication. The point here is therefore not to select one 'perhaps' at the cost of the other. That, we have seen above, is in any case logically impossible. The point is to retain both. And this means that the tensions between Supiot and Foucault's work beckon one to infer from them the fundamentally and interminably interrupted status of legal personality. The legal person exists as an interface between two eventualities, two 'perhapses'. It exists as neither the one, nor the other, but as both 'perhapses'. In other words, the legal person should be considered a self-interruption, an interruption of itself and thus of selfhood. It is torn between a concern with the noble dignity of the Enlightenment subject (which according to Kantian ethics must act against its own nature) and Goya's *Idiot*. And it is impossible to say which one of these two eventualities grants it superior autonomy and dignity.

There is, however, an observation regarding the specificity of human autonomy and dignity that the interrogation of the interruption of human and legal subjectivity in this chapter appears to render less unsayable. If it is true that the comparability of artificial intelligence and human subjectivity has raised one of the most pertinent epistemological and ontological questions of our time; and if it is likewise true that one of the most pertinent legal theoretical questions of our time concerns the attributability of legal subjectivity to artificial intelligence (see Chopra & White, 2004, 2011; Teubner, 2018) one may well consider the interruption of legal subjectivity outlined in this chapter the most obvious and most irreducible obstacle in the way of such comparison and attribution, for it is hardly thinkable that any programmable intelligence can be programmed to be so profoundly at odds with itself as the human subject appears to be.

ACKNOWLEDGEMENTS

Thanks are due to Claudio Novelli for helpful research assistance in the field of artificial intelligence law.

REFERENCES

Agamben, G. (2009). *What is an apparatus? And other essays*. Stanford, CA: Stanford University Press.

Allen, A. (1998). Foucault's debt to Hegel. *Philosophy Today*, *42*(1), 71–78.

Audier, S. (2015). *Penser le néolibéralisme. Le moment néolibéral, Foucault et la crise du socialisme*. Lormont: Le Bord de l'eau.

Bartl, W., Papilloud, C., & Terracher-Lipinski, A. (2019). Governing by numbers – Key indicators and the politics of expectations. An introduction. *Historical Social Research/Historische Sozialforschung*, *44*(2), 7–43.

Butler, J. (1999). *Subjects of desire: Hegelian reflections in twentieth century France*. New York, NY: Columbia University Press.

Chopra, S., & White, L. (2004). *Artificial agents—Personhood in law and philosophy*. In *Proceedings of ECAI*. Amsterdam: IOS Press.

Chopra, S., & White, L. (2011). *A legal theory for autonomous artificial agents*. Ann Arbor: University of Michigan Press.

Derrida, J. (1967). *De la Grammatologie*. Paris: Éditions de Minuit.

Diaz-Bone, R. (2015) Institutionalist and methodological perspectives on law – Contributions of the economics of convention. *Historical Social Research/Historische Sozialforschung*, *40*(1), 23–41.

Dujarier, M.-A. (2010). L'automatisation du jugement sur le travail. Mesurer n'est pas évaluer. *Cahiers Internationaux de Sociologie, Nouvelle Série*, *128–129*, 135–159.

Esposito, R. (2012). *Third person*. Cambridge: Polity Press.

Foucault, M. (1966). *Les Mots et les Choses*. Paris: Gallimard.

Foucault, M. (1971). *L'ordre du discours. Leçon inaugurale au Collège de France prononcée le 2 décembre 1970*. Paris: Gallimard.

Foucault, M. (1972). *Histoire de la Folie à l'âge Classique*. Paris: Gallimard.

Foucault, M. (1975). *Surveiller et punir*. Paris: Gallimard.

Foucault, M. (1986). *La pensée de dehors*. Montpellier: Fata Morgana.

Foucault, M. (2002). *Power – Essential works 1954–1984* (Vol. 3). London: Penguin Books.

Gündoğdu, A. (2015). *Rightlessness in an age of rights. Hannah Arendt and the contemporary struggles of migrants*. New York, NY: Oxford University Press.

Gutting, G. (2010). Foucault, Hegel and Philosophy. In T. O'Leary & C. Falzon (Eds.), *Foucault and philosophy* (pp. 17–35). Oxford: Wiley-Blackwell.

Haroche, C. (2010). L'inévaluable dans une société de défiance. *Cahiers Internationaux de Sociologie, Nouvelle Série*, *128–129*, 53–78.

Hegel, G. W. F. (1970a). Differenz des Fichteschen und Schellingschen Systems der Philosophie. In *Werke in Zwanzig Bänden* (Vol. 2). Frankfurt a. M.: Suhrkamp.

Hegel, G. W. F. (1970b). Grundlinien der Philosophie des Rechts. In *Werke in Zwanzig Bänden* (Vol. 7). Frankfurt a. M.: Suhrkamp.

Hegel, G. W. F. (1970c). Phänomenologie des Geistes. In *Werke in 20 Bänden* (Vol. 3). Frankfurt a. M.: Suhrkamp.

Jameson, F. (2009). *Valences of the dialectic*. New York, NY: Verso.

Jonas, E. (2015). Historicity and alterity: Revisiting the Foucault–Derrida debate. *Constellations*, *22*(4), 586–598.

Künzel, W. (1985). *Foucault liest Hegel*. Frankfurt a. M.: Haag + Herchen.

Lypp, B. (1978). Über die Wurzeln dialektischer Begriffsbildung in Hegels Kritik and Kants Ethik. In R.-P. Horstmann (Ed.), *Seminar: Dialektik in der Philosophie Hegels*. Frankfurt a. M.: Suhrkamp Verlag.

Muldoon, J. (2014). Foucault's forgotten Hegelianism. *Parrhesia*, *21*, 102–112.

Rohrmoser, G. (1961). *Subjektivität und Verdinglichung. Theologie und Gesellschaft im Denken des jungen Hegels*. Gütersloh: Gerd Mohn.

Riedel, M. (1975). Hegels Begriff der bürgerlichen Gesellschaft und das Problem seines geschichtlichen Ursprungs. In M. Riedel (Ed.), *Materialien zu Hegels Rechtsphilosophie* (pp. 247–275). Frankfurt a.M.: Suhrkamp.

Ritter, J. (2003). *Metaphysik und Politik*. Frankfurt a. M.: Suhrkamp.

Sembou, E. (2015). *Hegel's phenomenology and Foucault's genealogy*. Farnham: Ashgate.

Supiot, A. (2005) *Homo juridicus*. Paris: Seuil.

Supiot, A. (2010). *L'esprit de Philadelphie*. Paris: Seuil.

Supiot, A. (2015). *La Gouvernance par les nombres*. Paris: Fayard.

Teubner, G. (2018). Digitale Rechtssubjekte? Zum privatrechtlichen Status autonomer Softwareagenten. *Ancilla Iuris*, 35–78.

Van der Walt, J. (2019). *The concept of liberal democratic law*. London: Routledge.

CHAPTER 4

INTERRUPTING THE LEGAL PERSON: THINKING RESPONSIBILITY WITH HANNAH ARENDT

Jennifer L. Culbert

ABSTRACT

In this chapter, Arendt's reflections on the question of personal responsibility are taken as a discussion of 'interrupting the legal person'. Examining trials that took place after World War II, Arendt observes in 'Some Questions of Moral Philosophy', 'What the courts demand ... is that the defendants should not have participated' (pp. 33–34). Following Arendt, the author argues that thinking could have enabled possible perpetrators of great evil to meet this demand, for when a person stops to think, whatever they are doing is interrupted. What is more, the person who stops to think is themselves interrupted by thinking. In brief, becoming aware of the possibility that they exist as a person in a mode other than what Ngaire Naffine calls 'the responsible subject', thinking disrupts the legal person. A discussion of thinking as interrupting the legal person thus illuminates not only what may turn a person away from participation in the life of a criminal state, but also what that turn means for responsibility.

Keywords: Hannah Arendt; legal person; thinking; responsibility; accountability; complicity

Interrupting the Legal Person
Studies in Law, Politics, and Society, Volume 87A, 49–71

Published under exclusive licence by Emerald Publishing Limited
ISSN: 1059-4337/doi:10.1108/S1059-433720220000087A004

'Stop and think'. This familiar phrase calls attention to a characteristic feature of the activity of thought: thinking interrupts. In much of the work that follows her account of the trial of Adolf Eichmann, Hannah Arendt (1964) reflects on the significance of this feature. At Eichmann's trial, Arendt was struck by the 'shallowness' of the defendant, by the conventionality of his behavior, and his habit of using clichés to express himself. Listening to Eichmann and reading his personal account of the circumstances that led him to be accused in an Israeli courtroom of being the architect of 'the Final Solution', it occurred to Arendt that ordinary thoughtlessness and the human capacity to do extraordinary evil might be related. In the years that followed, she often wondered how thinking might help people avoid 'the banality of evil'. As she puts it in the first volume of *The Life of the Mind* (Arendt, 1978a),

> Could the activity of thinking as such, the habit of examining whatever happens to come to pass or to attract attention, regardless of results and specific content, could this activity be among the conditions that make men abstain from evil-doing or even actually 'condition' them against it? (p. 5)

In other words, might stopping to think interrupt a person who is acting badly or who is habituated to acting in such a manner?

In this chapter, I take Arendt's (2003a) reflections on thinking, specifically thinking under conditions when 'the majority or my whole environment has prejudged the issue' (p. 18) as a discussion of 'interrupting the legal person'. Under these conditions, a person can turn neither to social norms nor to the law for guidance about how to 'abstain from evil-doing'; on the contrary, social and legal conventions may support this kind of behaviour. Nevertheless, in postwar trials, the courts hold people responsible for participating in crimes that have been legalised by the government; in other words, the courts hold people responsible for things they do under conditions that make it difficult for them to appreciate that what they are doing is wrong.

Observing these conditions, Arendt states, 'What the courts demand … is that the defendants should not have participated' (pp. 33–34). This chapter begins with a discussion of this statement. Specifically, I consider how Arendt supposes it is possible for people not to participate in the behaviour postwar courts condemn. As many readers of Arendt's work have observed, Arendt wonders if the answer lies in thinking.[1] Arendt speculates that thinking may prevent someone from taking part in an activity that they have no other apparent way to know is wrong. Thinking may prevent them from taking part in that activity by virtue of the fact that thinking can cause them to experience some inconsistency in themselves that they cannot abide when they reflect on what they are doing.[2] To avoid that experience, they may then retreat from society. By contrast to Arendt, in this chapter, I suggest the relevant aspect of thinking is *not* the way in which it draws the thinker's attention to internal conflicts that may only be resolved when they don't participate in political society. I argue instead the politically significant aspect of thinking is that thinking simply interrupts 'normal' life.

While this interpretation of the power of thought may sound trivialising, it does not belittle Arendt's reflections on thinking. Rather, it takes seriously

Arendt's (1978a) claim that we live in an appearing world (p. 21). What is more, it allows us to consider more seriously the implications of Arendt's reflections on thinking for the question of responsibility. Arendt states,

> the simple truth of the matter is that only those who withdrew from public life altogether, who refused political responsibility of any sort, could avoid becoming implicated in crimes, that is, could avoid legal and moral responsibility. (p. 34)

In the rest of the chapter, I consider this statement and explore how withdrawal may be conceived as a responsible act.[3] Arendt may be interpreted as suggesting we may have a duty or a responsibility to think in order to avoid participating in evil.[4] However, in the text I have just cited, Arendt does not suggest that the thinker acts responsibly when they withdraw from public life; on the contrary, she observes that people 'refuse' and 'avoid' responsibility when they turn their backs on the state. Thus, a discussion of thinking illuminates not only what Arendt says postwar trial courts demanded of defendants but also how demanding that people think 'poses considerable problems precisely with respect to the question of responsibility' (Arendt, 2003a, p. 34)

Scholars have framed discussions of these 'considerable problems' in terms of Arendt's treatment of the difference between civil disobedience and conscientious objection.[5] In this chapter, I draw instead on Arendt's observations about the way thinking interrupts normal life. These observations call attention to how the person who thinks is *themselves* interrupted by thinking. That is to say, thinking exposes the thinker to the possibility that they exist as a person in a mode other than that which Ngaire Naffine (2003) calls 'the responsible subject' (p. 362). In this other mode, the person affects and is affected by others – human and otherwise – in relations that exceed 'calculable responsibility' (Satkunanandan, 2015, p. 2). This insight need not, however, lead us to embrace (negative) nihilism and dismiss life as we know it on the grounds that there are no grounds for determining, to use Michael Rothberg's (2019) language, 'victims and perpetrators'. Therefore, I conclude this chapter by describing how responsibility may be demonstrated in the act of walking away.

1. WHAT COURTS DEMAND

In the District Court in Jerusalem, Adolf Eichmann was accused of having committed horrific crimes, including crimes against the Jewish people, crimes against humanity, and war crimes. In her report on Eichmann's trial, Arendt (1964) notes that Eichmann stood accused of committing these crimes 'together with others' (p. 21). Eichmann responded to each count with the same plea: 'Not guilty in the sense of the indictment' (p. 21). After trying to determine in what sense Eichmann might have thought he was guilty, Arendt speculates that if it had been acknowledged that what Eichmann had done was a crime only in retrospect, he might have pleaded guilty to being an accessory to murder (p. 24). Although Eichmann insisted that he never killed anyone, he said he did not want

> to be one of those who now pretended that 'they had always been against it,' whereas in fact they had been very eager to do what they were told to do. (p. 24)

However, while he was aware of what he did, Eichmann insisted that he never acted 'out of base motives and in full knowledge of the criminal nature of his deeds' (p. 25). In fact, even though he was ordered to ship millions of men, women, and children to their death, Eichmann claimed he 'would have had a bad conscience only if he had not done what he had been ordered to do' (p. 25). In brief, Eichmann intended to do what he did but he never intended to do anything wrong.

According to Arendt, the judges in Eichmann's case assumed that the defendant 'like all "normal persons", must have been aware of the criminal nature of his acts' (p. 26). In the chapter, 'Personal Responsibility Under Dictatorship,' Arendt (2003a) observes that not only these judges but judges in all postwar trials shared a 'rather optimistic view of human nature' (p. 41) according to which a person has only to consult 'a "feeling of lawfulness" deep within themselves' (p. 40) to recognise the criminal nature of a particular order. Conscious of 'the very foundations of their profession', the judges in the Jerusalem trial could not admit that 'an average, "normal" person, neither feeble-minded nor indoctrinated nor cynical, could be perfectly incapable of telling right from wrong' (Arendt, 1964, p. 26).

The judges' view of human nature may have been due not only to their positive regard for their fellow man – the judges in Eichmann's trial were, Arendt suggests, perhaps 'too good' (p. 26) – but also because, as Arendt (2003b) remarks in the chapter 'Some Questions of Moral Philosophy', 'the admission that we change our minds about moral matters is very serious' (p. 84). In other words, the judges may have hesitated to admit we change our minds about moral matters out of fear of having to admit there is no given 'right' and 'wrong' that a person may always sense and refer to when they do not know what is the proper thing to do. To admit such a thing is to acknowledge 'what is right' has no natural or, to use Nietzschean (1990) language, 'real' existence (p. 50). Such an admission is serious; according to Arendt (2003b), moral matters are 'the greatest' (p. 84). But in addition, if such important matters may not be assumed to have the character of reality or a truth given by nature, disputes about them may never be settled or may be settled only temporarily. In her discussion of this point, Arendt cites Plato's *Laws*:

> 'men are perpetually disputing about rights and altering them, and whatever alteration they make at any time is at that time authoritative, owing its existence to artifice and legislation, and not in any way to nature (*Laws* 889e–890a)'. (cited pp. 84–85)

In brief, all laws 'are by convention only, and … conventions change from place to place and from time to time' (p. 84).[6]

When 'what is right' is recognised to be a matter of (changing) convention, the assumption that intent to do wrong is necessary for the commission of a crime is challenged (p. 277). Eichmann might declare, as Arendt suggests he does, that all his life he did not simply obey the law but abided by it because he understood it was his duty to do so. Eichmann claimed to have lived his whole life according to precepts taken from Kant, or rather 'the version of Kant "for the household use of the little man"' (Arendt, 1964, p. 136), which demand that a man 'go beyond the mere call of obedience and identify his own will with the principle behind the law – the source from which the law sprang' (pp. 136–137). As Arendt points out, for Kant that source was practical reason but for Eichmann, and for other law-abiding Germans during the Third Reich, 'the source from which the law sprang was the will of the Führer' (p. 137). Hence, the judges in Jerusalem may have been confronted with a person who 'never realized what he was doing' (p. 287). In the trial of Adolf Eichmann, the prosecution recognised as much when they sought to prove that Eichmann was guilty of murder by his own hand, an intentional killing that would have established Eichmann had committed a crime that he recognised as such (p. 22).

At least at first blush, Arendt's own solution to the problem of intention in her report on Eichmann's trial is unsatisfying. Assuming the voice of a judge on the court who is addressing Eichmann directly, Arendt states:

> There still remains the fact that you have carried out, and therefore actively supported, a policy of mass murder. For politics is not like the nursery; in politics obedience and support are the same. (p. 279)

In brief, Arendt does not deny Eichmann's argument that his only intention was to do his duty. What she condemns him for are his actions – the fact that he obediently carried out a policy of mass murder. That is to say, she does not concern herself with his knowledge of wrongdoing, his *mens rea* or guilty mind. Instead, she focusses on what he does. Or, more precisely, she focusses on what he does not do. Again, Arendt (2003a) says the courts required defendants 'not to have participated in crimes legalized by the government' (p. 34). Eichmann may be condemned because he did not *not* take part.

This solution to the problem of intention is unsatisfying, at least in part, because it seems to beg the question: if we grant that Eichmann was a well-intentioned and law-abiding citizen of Germany during World War II, and 'it was nothing more than misfortune' (Arendt, 1964, p. 279) that put him in a position to play a significant role in carrying out a policy of mass murder, we may not hold him responsible for what he did. But how then can we hold him responsible for what he did *not* do? In other words, on what grounds is it possible to consider nonparticipation as 'a legal standard for right and wrong' (Arendt, 2003a, p. 34)?

Arendt's response to this challenge is matter-of-fact. 'The simple truth' is, she says, 'only those who withdrew from public life altogether, who refused political responsibility of any sort, could avoid becoming implicated in crimes, that is could, avoid legal and moral responsibility' (p. 34). In brief, she does not attempt to justify a legal standard for right and wrong but simply states that the only way to avoid becoming implicated in the commission of a crime in Nazi Germany was not to take part in public life.

But this line of argument raises another question. What moved some people to withdraw from public life? To put the question another way, what failed to move so many? After studying Eichmann, Arendt suggests a possible answer. It is possible to act without ill intentions but nevertheless to do evil things when one acts without thinking.

According to Arendt (2003b), thinking means to examine and to question (p. 103). While the history of philosophy suggests that thinking requires either some superior kind of character or intelligence (Arendt, 1978a, p. 13), Arendt disagrees. She insists thinking is an activity of which everyone is capable (p. 13). Thus, thinking is neither a matter of wickedness or goodness, nor of intelligence or stupidity (p. 13). Also, thinking does not require or seek knowledge (p. 14). In order to think, it is not necessary to know something already nor is it supposed that knowledge is the goal. In addition, thinking is not a means to an end. In other words, thinking is not undertaken for a reason. Instead, thinking is undertaken for its own sake. It does not answer questions or come up with solutions to problems. In fact, it produces nothing useful. Thinking simply happens; it takes place, or more accurately time, inserting an interval or a pause in the everyday.[7] Thinking can arise out of any event or experience (Arendt, 2003b, p. 93). It occurs, Arendt says,

> when I, having watched an incident in the street or having become implicated in some occurrence, now start considering what has happened, telling it to myself as a kind of story. (p. 93)

The interruption of thought is a destructive affair, however, as it always involves the shattering of idols (Arendt, 2003b, p. 103). Thinking 'dissolves normal, positive concepts into their original meanings,' and shows negative 'concepts' to be in their origin nothing, meaningless (Arendt, 2003c, p. 179). Thus, Arendt says, the Athenians told Socrates 'that thinking was subversive, that the wind of thought was a hurricane which sweeps away all the established signs by which men orient themselves in the world' (p. 178). The wind of thought is so devastating because 'conventions, the rules and standards by which we usually live, don't show up too well under examination' (Arendt, 2003b, p. 104). Thus, when people who hold to rules and standards unthinkingly engage in the thinking process, they may be deprived of what they had taken for granted and on which they had relied to remain constant (p. 104). When this happens, thinking 'brings disorder into the cities and it confuses the citizens' (Arendt, 2003c, p. 178).[8]

Indeed, when you emerge from the place (or time) of thought you appear 'no longer sure of what had seemed to you beyond doubt while you were unthinkingly engaged in whatever you were doing' (p. 176). You are momentarily paralysed due to the fact that thinking not only 'relentlessly dissolves and examines anew all accepted doctrines and rules' but also 'can at every moment turn against itself, as it were, produce a reversal of the old values, and declare these as "new values"' (p. 177). In brief, when thinking itself is interrupted and you are abruptly brought back to your senses, you are at least temporarily unable to act as you have lost your bearings in the world you share with others. For even if thinking has undermined the foundations of common standards and norms of behaviour on which you have more or less knowingly relied and erected others in their place, Arendt (2003b) insists thinking itself 'will never tell you what to do, only prevent you from doing certain things, even though they are done by everybody around you' (p. 105).

Thinking is helpfully illuminated by Arendt's discussion of its opposite, non-thinking. First, by shielding people against the dangers of examination, non-thinking

> teaches them to hold fast to whatever the prescribed rules of conduct may be at a given time in a given society. What people then get used to is not so much the content of the rules, a close

> examination of which would always lead them into perplexity, as the possession of rules under which to subsume particulars. In other words, they get used to never making up their minds. (p. 178)

From this follows a second danger of nonthinking.

> If somebody then should show up who, for whatever reasons and purposes, wished to abolish the old 'values' or virtues, he will find it easy enough provided he offers a new code, and he will need no force and no persuasion – no proof that the new values are better than the old ones – to establish it. (p. 178)

In sum,

> Unfortunately, it seems to be much easier to condition human behavior and to make people conduct themselves in the most unexpected and outrageous manner, than it is to persuade anybody to learn from experience ...; that is, to start thinking and judging instead of applying categories and formulas which are deeply ingrained in our mind, but whose basis of experience has long been forgotten .... (Arendt, 2003a, p. 37)

Yet the absence of thinking is an ordinary experience of everyday life. Basically, Arendt (1978a) says, we do not have time, let alone the inclination, to stop and think (p. 4). We are habituated to prejudgements, and for this Arendt, perhaps surprisingly, does not condemn us. Instead, she acknowledges,

> Clichés, stock phrases, adherence to conventional, standardized codes of expression and conduct have the socially recognized function of protecting us against reality, that is, against the claim on our thinking attention that all events and facts make by virtue of their existence. If we were responsive to this claim all the time, we would soon be exhausted. (p. 4)

Nevertheless, under circumstances when most people are not alerted to the claim on their thinking attention that events and facts make, some people do sense this claim. And it is Arendt's (2003c) belief that 'in the rare moments when the chips are down', thinking attention may prevent catastrophes (p. 189). According to Arendt, while 'it does not create values, it will not find out, once and for all what "the good" is, and it does not confirm but rather dissolves accepted rules of conduct' (p. 188), thinking does liberate the faculty of judgement that enables people to say 'this is wrong' (p. 189).

As many readers note, Arendt is understandably tentative when she speculates that thinking may prevent catastrophes. Indeed, the tone of the whole discussion changes as Arendt presents her idea – or perhaps more accurately, her wish – that thinking has this power. Like Socrates at the end of the *Phaedo*, Arendt recognises that what she says cannot be demonstrated to be true. Nevertheless, she shares her idea with friends and followers, as much to console them as they struggle to reconcile themselves to a great loss as to persuade them that she is right. Those gathered at Socrates' death bed in the *Phaedo* confront having to live in a world without the philosopher while Arendt's readers must contend with the passing of the assumption that a 'normal' person is always capable of telling right from wrong.

The tale Arendt tells may comfort some of her readers and perplex others, but it may also, I suggest, obscure how thinking does, on Arendt's own account, exercise power in a setting where people are given no way to question what they do.

To shed some light on the power of thinking, I return to Arendt's description of the appearance of thought. As Arendt notes, all that can be observed of thought in an appearing world is an interruption of the normal conduct of people's lives. The unpredictable *effects* of thinking – specifically, the hoped-for liberation of the faculty of judgement that enables people to say 'this is wrong' – are not visible.[9] But the absence of evidence of these effects need not lead to the conclusion that when thinking happens nothing occurs. Indeed, the absence of these effects may suggest that whatever consequences thinking has, including perhaps the prevention of catastrophes, these consequences are due to the fact that 'Whenever we think, we stop whatever else we may have been doing' (Arendt, 2003b, p. 105).[10]

Of course, we may stop without thinking. The point I am making here does not, however, require that whenever someone withdraws from public life they do so because they have begun to think. It is important only to acknowledge that thought may be what interrupts and that thought may interrupt without necessarily revealing or realising some interior process or product. In other words, to the extent that thinking interrupts 'normal' politics, this interruption alone may change what seemed an inevitable course of events and start something new.

But how does stopping and withdrawing generate something new? It is necessary to show how under some circumstances, to not act is actually to do something (and to *not* not act is to do something wrong). In this context, consider Arendt's discussion of truth and politics. In that discussion, Arendt (2006) claims telling facts is a nonevent because it 'leads to no action whatever' (p. 246). In other words, according to Arendt, to tell facts is not to do anything for action introduces something new into the world and to tell facts 'tends under normal circumstances toward the acceptance of things as they are' (p. 246). However, under circumstances that are *not* normal, for instance, when 'a community has embarked upon organized lying on principle' (p. 247), Arendt insists the truthteller, whether they know it or not, has begun to act. They have begun to act because under the circumstances, the mere telling of facts starts them 'toward changing the world' (p. 247). Like the truthteller, I suggest, when we stop what we are doing, when we withdraw and no longer participate in public life, under certain circumstances we may begin to act. Under certain circumstances, such as the circumstances that pertained in Nazi Germany, the interruption of 'things as they are' may initiate something new. What Arendt describes as refusing political responsibility may then register as a political act.[11]

2. THE LEGAL PERSON

Conceiving of the significance of stopping to think in these terms allows us to approach from a new angle the issue of political responsibility that Arendt raises. For thinking does not only interrupt 'normal' politics; it also interrupts the person who thinks. Arendt describes how thinking perplexes the person who engages in it but she does not develop the implications of this insight for the 'normal' person who is held accountable at law and the grounds upon which their accountability is established.

While the term 'person' is often used in and by the law, it is not necessarily obvious who or what this 'person' is. As a note (2001) in the *Harvard Law Review* observes, courts rely on assumptions about personhood but they are not inclined to explain how they come to hold them or justify them. Consequently, how legal personhood is understood in a particular case appears to be determined by the judge who selects 'whatever theories of personhood suit the outcomes they desire' (p. 1759). According to the note, when law refers to the 'person' then, it alludes not to a coherent theory of personhood but to a metaphor that 'acts as a vehicle for expressing beliefs and values about persons, both legal and natural' (p. 1761).[12] Given how socially divisive beliefs and values about persons are – the note discusses the rhetoric of personhood in the slaveholding antebellum South as well as contemporary debates about abortion and corporate personhood – the note concludes that the courts' treatment of legal personhood 'communicates anxiety not only about divisive social issues, but also about the operation of law itself' (p. 1766). In the US context, the source of this anxiety is the interpretation and application of very fundamental notions of status. To the extent that 'person' is a status conferred on someone or something that ascribes to them some transcendent meaning, law hesitates to rule on the question of the person in any single, definitive way.

Against this backdrop, Ngaire Naffine (2003) intervenes to provide some 'order and clarity' to the field. In 'Who are Law's Persons?: From Cheshire Cats to Responsible Subjects,' Naffine surveys different branches of law that explicitly but more often implicitly discuss legal personality, and identifies three distinct versions of the 'person.' She calls the first version, 'P1', 'the Cheshire Cat'. P1 is the legal person who is understood to exist only because it is useful to law for there to be such an entity (p. 351). A legal person is therefore simply something law has endowed with a formal capacity to bear a right or duty; thus, it is 'a pure abstraction, not a thing or being' (p. 352). Although we often talk about legal persons as moral subjects of rights, Naffine explains, 'There is nothing or no-one which bears the rights and duties which constitute someone or something as a person in law' (p. 353). The legal person is therefore 'wholly formal' (H. Kelsen, cited p. 353), no more, in the words of Bryant Smith, 'than the smile of the Cheshire Cat after the cat had disappeared' (cited p. 353).

By contrast, the second version of the legal person Naffine identifies, 'P2', is definitely a human being. This legal person is 'linked with biological and also metaphysical definitions of humanity' (p. 357), and is often understood to have a strong spiritual dimension as well as an essence that may be described scientifically. As Naffine notes,

> What counts as a legal biological human is therefore not just subject to medical (which of course are also cultural) determinations about the beginnings and ends of a human being. What it means to be a biological legal human is also influenced by cultural ideas of what it is to be a whole and proper metaphysical person. (pp. 359–360)

Therefore, in western liberal legal culture, where the autonomy of the each human being is highly valued, legal persons are posited to be 'whole, integrated and individuated beings', that are 'separate and distinct and ideally self-possessing' (p. 360).

Finally, the third legal person Naffine identifies is 'the responsible subject', 'P3' (p. 362). P3 is

> both an intelligent agent and a moral agent in the sense that he is accountable for his actions. He can be held both morally and legally accountable for his actions because his actions are guided by reason: he knows what he is doing and still chooses to act as he does. (p. 362)

To the extent that this person can be understood to be free to act in ways which only affect himself, Naffine argues that P3, like P2, must be individuated and self-contained. But unlike P2, P3 is first and foremost a person not because he is a biological or spiritual being but because he is a reasonable one who is capable of rationally choosing his course of action (p. 364).

According to Naffine, 'P3 has had a profound and pervasive influence on legal thought; he represents to many the ideal (if not the actual) legal actor' (p. 364). Other scholars Naffine cites support this claim. David Brown and his co-authors of *Criminal Laws* state, 'Traditional criminal legal doctrine constructs a free-willed, intentional, rational, choosing, responsible, individual subject: a subject morally suitable for punishment' (cited p. 364); Waller and Williams declare,

> almost the whole of our system of substantive criminal law is based upon the view that a human being is a rational creature, free to choose how to act, and deserving of punishment if she or he chooses to act immorally or wickedly. (cited p. 364)

As we have seen, Arendt (1964) suggests that in the postwar trials judges share this view of a human being insofar as they expect to encounter 'an average, "normal" person, neither feeble-minded nor indoctrinated nor cynical' who is capable of telling right from wrong and is aware of the criminal nature of their acts (p. 26). In brief, they assume the defendant to be a responsible person who not only has the capacity to know but the capacity to will what he does.

When Arendt describes the disruptive effects of thought, these capacities do not necessarily disappear. However, she does not stop to consider that when a responsible person stops to think, that is to say, when the legal person is interrupted, these capacities are no longer their own. Instead, they are shared by the *persons* the legal person becomes. The legal person's capacities for knowing and willing are shared because thinking pluralises the legal person. When we think, Arendt (2003b) says, 'we find that we are in company, in the company of ourselves' (p. 96). In brief, when we think we find we are not one alone but ourselves with others. In effect, the legal person who stops to think discovers they are not an individual, solitary, and sovereign, but an (often-times unruly) assembly.[13]

To put the point plainly, I am suggesting that when Arendt (2003c) claims thinking 'has a destructive and undermining effect on all established criteria, values, measurements for good and evil, in short, on those customs and rules of conduct we treat of in morals and ethics' (p. 176), one of the most easily overlooked commonplaces of morals and ethics that may be undermined is the notion that the thinker is a single individual. Arendt says as much herself but she does not, as it were, think through what she observes. According to Arendt (1978a), there are not many thinkers who describe or examine their own thinking experience (p. 168). Socrates is one the few, so she turns to him for insight into *dianoeisthai* or what it is 'to think a matter through' (Arendt, 2003b, p. 91). In the *Theaetetus*, Socrates explains *dianoeisthai* is 'a discourse that the mind carries on with itself about any subject it is considering' (cited p. 91). In this discourse, 'the mind asks itself questions and answers them, saying yes or no to itself' (cited p. 91). In other words, thinking is 'a dialogue between me and myself' (p. 119). For Arendt, what is significant about this dialogue is not the content of the exchange between me and myself but its character, or rather, its *characters* and the relationship between them. Arendt explains this significance in a discussion of the *Gorgias*. In the *Gorgias*, Socrates says to Callicles,

> It would be better for me that my lyre or a chorus directed should be out of tune and loud with discord, and that multitudes of men should disagree with me rather than that I, *being one*, should be out of harmony with myself and contradict me. (emphasis by Arendt, 2003c; cited p. 181)

In Arendt's reading of this statement, Socrates proposes something paradoxical. She notes,

> Socrates talks of being one and *therefore* not being able to risk getting out of harmony with himself. But nothing that is identical with itself, truly and absolutely *one* like A is A, can be either in or out of harmony with itself; you always need at least two tones to produce a harmonious sound. (p. 183)

In brief, Socrates claims he is an individual, 'one', but he also implies he is or can be more than one insofar as the one he claims he is can suffer discord, that is to say, can be out of tune or agreement with itself. To resolve this paradox, Arendt offers a proposition of her own: 'when I appear and am seen by others, I am one' but at the same time, 'I am also for myself' (p. 183).

Arendt's proposition resolves Socrates' paradox in the *Gorgias* by insisting that when I am for myself, 'I clearly am not just one. A difference is inserted into my Oneness' (p. 184). According to Arendt, I appear as one, a distinct, self-possessed individual, but I experience something else. What I experience is difference, variation, diversity, dissimilarity. I am not one. In other words, 'I contain multitudes' (Whitman, 1892, https://www.poetryfoundation.org/poems/45477/song-of-myself-1892-version).

To be sure, Arendt does not consistently recognise the implications of the insertion of difference she describes as being as multifarious as I suggest. Instead, Arendt claims,

> So long as I am conscious, that is, conscious of myself, I am identical with myself only for others to whom I appear as one and the same. For myself, articulating this being-conscious-of-myself, I am inevitably *two-in-one*. (p. 184)

But she does acknowledge that the other myself may be characterised in different ways. Citing Socrates in *Hippias Major*, Arendt (2003b) describes the other self as a 'very obnoxious fellow "who always cross-examines"' and as 'a close relative, living in the same house' (p. 186), as well as 'the friend' (citing Aristotle p. 98). In addition, Arendt observes,

> Human consciousness suggests that difference and otherness, which are such outstanding characteristics of the world of appearances as it is given to man as his habitat among a plurality of things, are the very conditions for the existence of man's ego as well. (p. 184)

And from this observation Arendt concludes, 'The curious thing that I am needs no plurality in order to establish difference; it carries the difference within itself when it says: "I am I"' (p. 184). In brief, according to Arendt, thinking reveals a fundamental feature of human being. Difference and otherness, which Arendt (2003c) describes as 'outstanding characteristics of the world of appearances as it is given to man for his habitat among a plurality of things' (p. 184), are not simply features of the world that lies between human beings, the world into which they are born and to which they contribute with the fabrication of things that may last, be seen, and be used (Arendt, 1958, p. 173). Difference and otherness are critical, constitutive elements of being 'one'; that is to say, one is not singular, self-possessed, sovereign, and solitary.

Again, capacities for self-determination and the like do not necessarily disappear when one stops to think. My suggestion is only that when a person stops to think, specifically, when the legal person is interrupted by thought, such capacities are no longer their own or theirs alone. Instead, they are shared by the *persons* the person becomes. In brief, thinking pluralises the legal person. Thus, when Arendt (2003c) claims that thinking 'has a destructive and undermining effect on all established criteria, values, measurements for good and evil, in short, on those customs and rules of conduct we treat of in morals and ethics' (p. 176), one of the most basic customs that may be challenged is the assumption that the thinker is an individual. When thinking interrupts the legal person, it disturbs their apparent singularity with the revelation that they are more than one.

3. RESPONSIBILITY

In light of this revelation, the problems posed by nonparticipation for the question of responsibility to which Arendt alludes in her discussion of postwar trials may be reformulated. As Naffine remarks, legal scholars assume 'P3' is the only *one* who can bear responsibility as both versions of the legal person P2 and P3 'come in ones, not twos' (p. 360). However, Arendt's reflections on thinking suggest that responsibility is never properly understood as the burden of any *one* to carry alone. In fact, responsibility is not a burden at all. It is not a burden because responsibility is not a delimited thing that can be carried, shifted, or laid down. Nor can it be measured and distributed so that those who are more blameworthy take on more than those who are less so. Rather, Arendt's description of thinking suggests responsibility is better understood as attentiveness to the others of which one is constituted and with which one lives.

Arendt (2003a) famously claims that those few who in all walks of life did not collaborate and refused to participate in public life under the Nazis differed from their neighbours only in that 'they dared to judge by themselves, and they were capable of doing so not because they disposed of a better system of values or because the old standards of right and wrong were still firmly planted in their mind and conscience' but because 'they asked themselves to what extent they would still be able to live in peace with themselves after having committed certain deeds; and they decided that it would be better to do nothing, not because the world would then be changed for the better, but simply because only on this condition could they go on living with themselves at all' (p. 44). As Arendt emphasises here, neither intuitive moral sense nor abstract reason directed the actions of the people who refused to participate in public life under the Nazis. Withdrawal is instead both the affect and the effect of thinking that reveals the plurality of the self, obliging an apparent one to contend with others. For Arendt (2003b) this means,

> the criterion of right and wrong, the answer to the question, what ought I to do? depends in the last analysis neither on habits and customs, which I share with those around me, nor on a command of either divine or human origin, but on what I decide with regard to myself. In other words, I cannot do certain things, because having done them I shall no longer be able to live with myself. (p. 97)

Arendt says here that to be able to live with oneself is to be able to find a modus vivendi with the others revealed to oneself in thinking. The thinker answers to these others, not as a subordinate to a superior nor as a student to a teacher, but as a note responds to or is inspired by other notes. One is summoned by others to strike a chord with them, playing off the differences between them in such a way as to make a satisfying (or perhaps just a 'good-enough') sound, a note one can live with.[14]

To find a balance in this way, one must be attentive to what is proposed or demanded by others. As Arendt (2003b) points out, thinking never tells one what to do (p. 105). Thus, harmony is achieved in the moment, its composition a function of the specific contributions of various interlocutors, never final and never perfect. From the ancient Greek *harmonia*, meaning 'agreement, concord of sounds', 'means of joining', and also 'settled government, order', related to *harmos* 'fastenings of a door; joint, shoulder', the word 'harmony' is often identified with the Greek goddess of concord and order. Drawing from Arendt's description of thinking, I propose that these elements are brought together not by a divine being but by material sensitivity and responsiveness to what appears within and beyond the thinker.[15] Such attentiveness allows the differences that become apparent with thought to come to be associated with one another in a way that is tolerable, perhaps even agreeable, at least for a while. This attentiveness is how I understand responsibility.

As Shalini Satkunanandan (2015) explains, responsibility may be defined as 'certain demands upon us that require a response' (p. 8). According to Satkunanandan, 'The requisite nature of these demands depends on a binding claim that is somehow different from force, habit, and interest (though it may coincide with them)' (p. 8). To explain the power of these demands to obligate, she turns to etymology and traces responsibility back to the Latin *respondere*: '"to respond", "to answer, to reply to", as well as "to promise in return", "to match, balance, correspond to, be equal to, resemble, measure up to"' (p. 8). She concludes that responsibility thus includes 'an understanding of the compelling demands upon us in terms of debts owed *and* also an understanding of these demands as requests for a response' (p. 8). According to Satkunanandan, many western philosophers identify 'being human' with 'inexhaustible responsibility' and recognize, therefore, the temptation to limit the notion of responsibility to 'a series of debts that can be identified in advance, reckoned up, negotiated, balanced out, and more or less discharged' (pp. 4–5) so that 'we can monitor our own and others' fulfillment of responsibilities' (p. 5). Satkunanandan calls this notion of responsibility 'calculable responsibility', which she contrasts with 'extraordinary responsibility'. The philosophers Satkunanandan discusses conceive of extraordinary responsibility in different ways but, she claims, they all recognise it as a 'constitutive call to attentiveness' (p. 6), a call that invites us to rise to 'the responsibility constitutive of our humanity' (p. 6).

As this call demands we confront our 'ontological condition', it is rarely answered (p. 6). Satkunanandan implies we are deterred by 'the extent to which relationships even beyond our relations with our intimates are also comprehensible through a gift framework or one of indeterminant reciprocity' (p. 6). Betraying the pervasive logic of calculable responsibility, it seems we are afraid of too much responsibility to attend fully to the situation at hand (p. 8).[16] To acknowledge what we are given by others and what we owe to them is to risk a sense of existential bankruptcy, a feeling that perhaps we are not the 'self-made' men we imagined ourselves to be and that we do not control sufficient resources to meet the demands of our ontological creditors.

Despite how horrifying this realisation may be, the concept of a primordial indebtedness is, nevertheless, appealing. Arendt certainly recognises the appeal. In the second volume of *Life of the Mind*, in a discussion of Martin Heidegger's analysis of the conscience and his turn to the figure of the thinker, Arendt (1978b) notes that in Heidegger's earlier work, the self, once summoned back to itself by the call of conscience, turns to 'a thinking that expresses gratitude that the "naked That" has been given at all' (p. 185).[17] As this attitude of 'thinking and thanking' may be seen as a variant of Plato's *thaumazein* (wonder), the beginning principle of philosophy, Arendt does not find it striking or surprising (p. 185). Indeed, she claims, 'we have only to think of Nietzsche's praise of the "Yes-sayers"' or read some of the century's great poets. She adds, 'They at least show how suggestive such affirmation can be as a solution for the apparent meaninglessness of an entirely secularised world' (p. 185). In other words, the sense of indebtedness that characterises 'calculable responsibility' expresses a rationale by which it is possible for the self to be guided when other principles and authority figures have disappeared.

Significantly, however, when Arendt herself poses the question, 'What makes us think?' she does not refer to Heidegger's 'idea of guilt' or his notion that human existence *owes* its existence to something that it is not itself (p. 184). Instead she turns to Plato's *Theaetetus*, specifically to the passage in which Socrates compliments Theaetetus for 'wondering', which is, Socrates claims 'the true mark of the philosopher' (Arendt, 1978a, cited p. 142). In a close reading of the passage that follows Socrates' remark, Arendt connects Theaetetus' puzzlement with the 'wonder-struck beholding' of men to whom a god, disguised as a familiar human being, appears (p. 142). As it is the god's appearance that occasions the beholding, Arendt concludes, 'responding wonder, therefore, is not something men can summon up by themselves; the wonder is a *pathos*, something to be suffered, not acted' (pp. 142–143). Arendt notes then that 'The wonder that is the starting-point of thinking is neither puzzlement nor surprise nor perplexity; it is an *admiring* wonder' (p. 143).

In brief, the compelling nature of the demand to respond that Satkunanandan, following Heidegger, identifies with a sense of gratitude and indebtedness is characterised by Arendt instead as 'admiration and willingness to affirm in thought' (p. 148). What compels the Greeks, she says, is admiration for 'the invisible harmony and beauty that bind together the infinite diversity of particular beings' (p. 149). Arendt does not explicitly subscribe to this view of the whole. Instead, she emphasises how the viewing, 'the wonder-struck beholding', is what moves people. In other words, regarding an appearance compels a response. 'Suffered' rather than 'summoned', the feeling of wonder at the sight of what appears demands a reply; it makes us think.[18] Thinking, Arendt says, again, 'inevitably has a destructive and undermining effect' (p. 176). But, she says, it also makes you fully awake and alive, so that you can see 'you have nothing in your hand but perplexities, and the most we can do with them is share them with each other' (p. 176). Indeed, in her reading of the passage from *Theatetus*, Arendt claims, 'What we marvel at is confirmed and affirmed by admiration which breaks out into speech' (p. 143). Wonder makes us (able to) speak; it makes us responsive and response-able.

To summarise, as I read Arendt's reflections on the question of personal responsibility, those who withdraw from public life are people who, literally, find themselves thinking. 'Normal' life is interrupted with a turn away from immediate experience to examine what is happening, what they are implicated in doing, how they are involved. This examination is undertaken in a conversation people are called to have with themselves. This conversation is not one in which they intend or will to take part; they are called to it by appearances that are at once familiar and suddenly astonishing. Wonder, a feeling of amazement and admiration, makes people think. It demands a response. The experience of this demand moves people and they find themselves – with the others of themselves – examining anew all that they had taken for granted or assumed to be certain, stable, or set, in light of what these others have to say. Engaged in this conversation, the responsible person stops participating in the activities of the society or state, thereby making manifest their ability to respond, their 'suffering' of awe at the appearance, the awfulness, of 'the manifold wonders at the world's sheer thereness' (Arendt, 1978a, p. 78) expressed in a bewildering and clarifying exchange with the others of themselves.

4. CONCLUSION

In a context where criminality is both pervasive and routinised, to identify the conduct of the few who refuse political responsibility of any sort as the norm or standard by which courts of law hold people responsible for their actions seems disingenuous (and desperate), taking advantage, as it does, of the slippage between two senses of the word 'standard.' Nonparticipation is the exception rather than the rule in a totalitarian society. As Arendt (2003a) herself remarks, in a society in which unequivocal acceptance of the ruling principles is demanded, anyone who occupies a position of any public significance at all, 'from advertising agencies to the judiciary, from play-acting to sports journalism, from primary and secondary schooling to the universities and learned societies' (p. 33), is implicated in one way or another in the deeds of the regime (p. 33). To refer to the few instances when people successfully withdraw from society as validating a principle by which others are held responsible for the deeds of the regime is to establish with a grammatical sleight of hand an improbable expectation – I called it a wish earlier – as a norm.

In my interpretation of Arendt's reflections on the question of personal responsibility, I suggest how such a 'standard' might be understood as something other than a frantic effort to affirm human nature and an innate human sense of lawfulness. However, my suggestion implies that the legal person at the centre of a trial, the person who Arendt (1964) insists 'must suffer for what he has done, not for what he has caused others to suffer' (p. 9), is not, properly speaking, a responsible person. Or rather, in my view, the legal person Naffine calls 'P3'or 'the responsible subject' is misnamed. For this subject is not responsible; they are *accountable*.

While responsibility and accountability are often used interchangeably, by distinguishing between them I mean to highlight the sense of accountability that remains from its etymological origins in the Old French *conter*, meaning 'to count, add up' as well as 'tell a story' (derived from the Latin *computare*, 'to count, sum up, reckon together', from *com*, 'with, together', and *putare*, 'to reckon', originally 'to prune' from *pau-*, 'to cut, strike, stamp'.) I highlight this sense of accountability in order to reiterate a point Naffine makes in her discussion of P3 that I have already emphasised; P3 is *one*. He is an individual, identical to himself at all times. Indeed, stressing this point herself, Naffine says,

> [P3] has been described as an undesirable caricature of a human being: impossibly self-possessed and self-reliant, will-driven, clinically rational and individualistic. Certainly he is never pregnant, for this would threaten his physical integrity. (p. 365)

In other words, the legal person is a figure prohibited from containing multitudes. He cannot be responsible then, for the responsible person, the person who thinks, is not identical to themselves. They are called to respond to those others with whom they live for they not only support them but are supported by them when they, more or less obnoxiously, challenge them to examine their comforting but facile conceits of autonomy and self-determination, among other accepted doctrines and rules.[19]

The autonomous, self-determining individual, the accountable *one*, allows law to satisfy the desire to find guilty and punish. In *Twilight of the Idols*, Nietzsche (1990) identifies this desire. Nietzsche associates accountability with the doctrine of will, the belief that in the act of willing, an act we witness in an 'inner world', we 'catch causality in the act' and establish it as 'a given fact' (p. 60). The establishment of this fact gives us the ability to trace a novel feeling or an unfamiliar exertion back to something certain. Nietzsche claims,

> To trace something unknown back to something known is alleviating, soothing, gratifying, and gives moreover a feeling of power. Danger, disquiet, anxiety attend the unknown – the first instinct is to *eliminate* these distressing states. (p. 62)

But more than this, to the extent that we can trace a state of being back to the will, 'to intentions, to accountable acts', we may insist that the origin of every action lies in the consciousness and thereby deprive becoming of its innocence (p. 64). With the doctrine of the will, when 'being in this or that state is traced back to will, to intentions, to accountable acts', one may be found guilty and one may be held accountable for how one becomes. Indeed, according to Nietzsche, 'the doctrine of the will has been invented essentially for the purpose of punishment, that is of finding guilty' (p. 64). Naffine's 'P3' exemplifies this doctrine. P3 knows what he is doing and chooses to do what he does, and because he knows and chooses, he is accountable for his actions (p. 362). Recall that according to the scholars Naffine cites, P3 is 'a subject morally suitable for punishment' and 'deserving of punishment if he or she chooses to act immorally or wickedly' (cited p. 364).

As we have seen, when nonparticipation in a criminal state is held up as a legal standard, the question of responsibility, or more precisely, suitability for punishment, becomes especially problematic. Consider, the doctrine of complicity. This body of doctrine determines one person is responsible for the crimes committed by another. The underlying assumption of the doctrine of complicity is that a person who willingly participates in furthering criminal conduct but does not actually commit a criminal act should be accountable to the same extent as the criminal actor. The only way to be excluded from criminal liability is for a person not only to withdraw from the criminal enterprise but also to act to thwart its success. The fact that one walks away demonstrates only that one has been in a criminal 'state', not that one has willed to leave it. To avoid punishment, one has to make this act of will apparent so that it can be counted.

Critics of the doctrine of complicity like Sara Mohamed and Melissa Murray take issue with this requirement. In a chapter on Ursula K. Le Guin's (1991) famous short story, 'The Ones Who Walk Away from Omelas', Mohamed and Murray (2017) argue that the doctrine of complicity 'undervalues the extraordinary exercise of will required to extract oneself from an environment of pervasive wrongdoing' (p. 229). According to Mohamed and Murray, the requirement of 'affirmative action' effects a contradiction that undermines the legitimacy of the doctrine of complicity. Criminal acts are understood as choices that are within the actor's control. Indeed, it is on the basis of this understanding that 'the state may fairly impose punishment, condemning the individual's poor choices and bad acts' (p. 232). That every criminal offence must result from an individual's voluntary act 'underscores the centrality of the individual actor's agency and autonomy to criminal responsibility' (p. 232). However, Mohamed and Murray point out, in the criminal law's account of what it means to walk away from a criminal enterprise, an individual actor's agency and autonomy is respected only insofar as they once chose to participate in that enterprise. In other words, the choice the actor makes to withdraw is not recognised as an act of volition, despite the strength of will it often takes to leave. In the case of Le Guin's short story, those who leave the state of Omelas depart a place of unusual prosperity, beauty, and delight. What is more, they leave without being able to imagine where they are going. However, Omelas is also a place where a horrifying bargain has been struck. The people of Omelas all understand their happiness and the quality of their lives depend wholly on the abuse and misery of a single lonely child kept captive in a filthy basement. Mohammed and Murray argue that 'The Ones Who Walk Away from Omelas' powerfully illustrates what criminal law overlooks: 'that it is incredibly difficult to walk away from situations in which everyone insists that wrongdoing is the right thing to do' (p. 229) and consequently, that law has an 'incomplete and impoverished understanding' of those who do withdraw (p. 229). Specifically, they say, law 'undervalues the extraordinary exercise of will required to extract oneself from an environment of pervasive wrong doing' (p. 229).

In this critique of the doctrine of complicity, Mohamed and Murray double down on the assumption that the people who withdraw are legal persons, individual actors who know and choose what they do. In order to affirm the moral quality of the withdrawal of these individuals from criminal enterprises, Mohamed and Murray assume retreat is the effect of an extraordinary act of will, an act of will that should be counted (positively) when the state judges them. However, Mohamed and Murray make this case without listening to their clients. That is to say, they fail to notice the silence of those who walk away.

> At times one of the adolescent girls or boys who go to see the child does not go home to weep or rage, does not, in fact, go home at all. Sometimes also a man or woman much older falls silent for a day or two, and then leaves home. These people go out into the street, and walk down the street alone. They keep walking, and walk straight out of the city of Omelas, through the beautiful gates. They keep walking across the farmlands of Omelas. Each one goes alone, youth or girl, man or woman. (Le Guin, 1991, p. 5)

To my ear, the silence of the youth or the girl, man or woman, who withdraws from life in Omelas simultaneously interrupts and makes manifest an interruption of the 'normal' person they once appeared to be. Thinking, perhaps, is the occasion of this interruption but, obviously, no account is provided. Those who walk away never explain why they go.[20] Thus, we may not ever know if thinking saves anyone from participating in 'the worst'. We may know only that the thinking person stops what they are doing. Perhaps they are shocked by what suddenly appears to them. Moved by wonder, received notions, old values, and familiar norms become strange. In responding to what suddenly appears to them, the thinker is revealed to be a multitude. Under such circumstances, nonparticipation is not an act of will; it is a reaction to a mundane experience or event, an everyday situation, that for no apparent reason and by no apparent means dissolves the persona of the legal person and calls for a reexamination of all that had been taken for granted. Made to think, the person finds themselves in the company of others, the others of themselves, the others of which and with which they must find a way to live if they are to go on. Together, but not necessarily without disagreement and discomfort, they are moved to disrupt what was settled and made to find or fashion another arrangement. Thus, thinking interrupts not only normal life but the normal person, the one who is held accountable, the legal person. This interruption throws everything into upheaval allowing us to harmonise otherwise and do something else.

NOTES

1. Some of these readers are collected in *Thinking in Dark Times: Hannah Arendt on Ethics and Politics*, edited by Roger Berkowitz, Jeffrey Katz, and Thomas Keenan (2010). Another collection of readers who observe and reflect on Arendt's discussion of thinking as a possible way to resist evil is gathered in *Power, Judgment and Political Evil*, edited by Andrew Schaap, Danielle Celermajer, and Vrasidas Karalis (2010).

2. Of course, as Paul Formasa (2010) notes, many people are willing 'to put up with some moral self-disapproval in order to get something they value more highly, be it wealth, power, revenge or pleasure. In any case, moral self-disapproval is often easy enough to get rid of through self-deception, rationalization, compartmentalization and gradual habituation' (p. 95).

3. Withdrawal conceived as a responsible act may be contrasted with 'opting out' as discussed by Bonnie Honig (2017), but more importantly with Bernard Williams's motto for integrity over compliance, 'Not through me!', that Honig also discusses (pp. 31–34).

4. Richard Bernstein (2000) warns that Arendt should not be misinterpreted on this score, however. According to Bernstein, Arendt never specifies 'necessary and sufficient conditions that can "prevent catastrophes"' (p. 285). In other words, Arendt offers no guarantees against evil. After a detailed discussion of the moral relevance of thought for Arendt, Deirdre Mahony (2018) ultimately reaches the same conclusion.

5. See, for example, Jennet Kirkpatrick (2017).

6. It is tempting then to use force – physical or philosophical – to end these disputes. According to Arendt (2003b), this is what Plato does in the *Laws* when he proposes that the laws be written down so they will be 'always at rest' (p. 85). While these laws will be man-made, and hence are not 'natural' and everlasting, because 'they are "at rest" and do not change' the multitude will end by believing they are given, fixed, and never-ending (p. 85).

7. Heath Massey (2011) argues that time is central in Arendt's analysis of thinking. Observing also how Arendt describes thinking as interrupting all other activities, Massey stresses that the assumption that withdrawal is a movement from one *place* to another is problematic. According to Massey, for Arendt 'the "place or region" of thought should not be understood spatially at all, but temporally. The question is not *where* we are when we think, but *when*' (p. 75). Drawing on Arendt's reading of Franz Kafka's parable 'HE', Massey claims, 'For Arendt, thinking is *not* a matter of transcending time to achieve a view from eternity, but of inhabiting the gap between past and future' (p. 77). Out of this gap a 'diagonal force' (citing 1978, p. 77) arises and a path 'paved by thinking' (citing 1978, p. 78) emerges. Massey says, 'This image of the "when we think" suits Arendt's purpose of describing the basic experience of thinking as a withdrawal from the business of life and ordinary time without committing the metaphysical fallacy of locating thought in another world' (p. 78). It also avoids falling prey to the wish to master the future (p. 87).

8. Nihilism may be opposed to thinking but thinking is easily blamed for nihilism. Indeed, Arendt (2003c) acknowledges, 'What we commonly call nihilism … is actually a danger inherent in the thinking activity itself' (p. 177). However, Arendt insists nihilism proper is not the product of thinking. Arendt observes: 'All critical examinations must go through a stage of at least hypothetically negating accepted opinions and "values" by finding out their implications and tacit assumptions, and in this sense nihilism may be seen as an ever-present danger of thinking' (p. 177). But Arendt argues this danger does not arise out of thinking. Thinking does not bring forth any new creed, she says (pp. 177–178). In any case, nihilism is opposed to thinking as it arises 'out of the desire to find results which would make further thinking unnecessary' (pp. 177–178). Indeed, insofar as nihilism remains bound to the 'so-called positive values' it negates, it is nothing other than 'the

other side of conventionalism' (p. 177). By contrast, 'Thinking is equally dangerous to all creeds' (pp. 177–178).

9. Jerome Kohn (2000) argues that a major task for Arendt is to find signs in the world that indicate the reality of mental processes. Indeed, he attributes the 'strangeness' of *The Life of the Mind* to Arendt's 'fidelity to the world at this level' (p. 161).

10. According to Arendt, we stop whatever we may have been doing because thinking, although occasioned by events and experiences in the world, always 'removes itself from what is present and close at hand' (p. 199). Arendt says, 'it is as though we moved into a different world' (p. 165). This withdrawal – observed throughout the history of philosophy and interpreted in terms of a two-world metaphysics that identifies (incorrectly) thinking with death and the activity of thinking with eternal contemplation of the Forms – makes manifest a turn away from immediate experience to the 'storehouse of memory'. Arendt (1978a) describes this turn also as a process of preparation, a process by which visible sense objects are transformed into thought objects as 'the mind actively and deliberately remembers, recollects, and selects from the storehouse of memory whatever arouses its interest sufficiently to induce concentration' (p. 77). So prepared the mind may not only learn how to deal with things that are absent but may also ready itself to '"go further", towards the understanding of things that are always absent, that cannot be remembered because they were never present to sense experience' (p. 77). As a result, the activity of thinking is always 'out of order'; it reflects without purpose and raises unanswerable questions, 'going beyond the natural curiosity awakened by the manifold wonders of the world's sheer thereness' (p. 78).

11. As noted above, like all action, what is begun is unpredictable. To act, Arendt (1958) famously says, 'means to take an initiative, to begin ..., to set something in motion' (p. 177). What is new is itself something unexpected, something which cannot be expected from whatever may have happened before (p. 178). But what is more, every act, even the smallest that occurs in the most limited circumstances, is characterised by what Arendt describes as 'boundlessness' (p. 190). An act is boundless because an actor moves always in relation to other acting beings (p. 190). Consequently, every action occasions a reaction which is itself an action as well as a response, striking out on its own and affecting others. Thus, 'one deed, and sometimes one word, suffices to change every constellation' (p. 190). Action and reaction can never be reliably confined to two people. This means the effects (and affects) of an act cannot be anticipated. 'This is not simply a question of inability to foretell all the logical consequences of a particular act', Arendt claims (p. 191). The unpredictability of action is also the result of the way in which action gives rise to stories, stories that are not told by the actors themselves but by storytellers who see what happens and try to share with others what is revealed to them. In sum, it is those who observe the interruption of 'normal' politics that tell the story rather than those who stop and think. What is more, the stories told of their withdrawal from the public world, the meanings made of their nonparticipation, may be surprising, for what is done is still effecting everything else.

12. In his discussion of legal fictions, Lon Fuller (1930–1931) reminds us that 'the word "person" originally meant "mask"; that its applications to human beings was at first metaphorical' (p. 377).

13. Bonnie Honig (1993) claims that 'Arendt agrees with Nietzsche that there is no essential self, no given unity awaiting discovery or realization' (p. 78). In other words, 'There is no being behind the doing' (p. 78). Identity is 'a hard won and not always well-fitting product of action' (p. 77). In *On Revolution*, Arendt (1965) suggests this product is a '*persona*' (pp. 96–97). In Latin, *persona* originally signified the mask ancient actors used to wear in a play (p. 97). In classical Rome, 'The distinction between a private individual in Rome and a Roman citizen, was that the latter had a persona, a legal personality' (p. 97). Appearing to echo Fuller (1930–1931), Arendt comments, 'The point was that "it is not the natural Ego which enters a court of law. It is a right-and-duty-bearing person, created by the law, which appears before the law"' (p. 97).

14. See Marianne Constable (2014).

15. For an elaboration of the manner in which elements are brought together in this way and 'the experience of being continuously subject to influence and still managing to add something to the mix', see Jane Bennett (2020).

16. The concern manifest in calculative responsibility is made abundantly clear in the logic of *McCleskey* v. *Kemp,* 481 U.S. 279 (1987) and is identified by Justice Brennan in his dissenting opinion at 339. ('The Court next states that its unwillingness to regard petitioner's evidence as sufficient is based in part on the fear that recognition of McCleskey's claim would open the door to widespread challenges to all aspects of criminal sentencing. *Ante* at 481 U.S. 314-315. Taken on its face, such a statement seems to suggest a fear of too much justice. ... The prospect that there may be more widespread abuse than McCleskey documents may be dismaying, but it does not justify complete abdication of our judicial role'.)

17. According to Arendt, in Heidegger's later work the thinker no longer listens to the call of conscience but instead listens to 'the call of Being'. In Arendt's words, 'the thinker is not summoned by himself to his Self', and this means that 'the Self no longer acts in itself ... but, obedient to Being' (p. 187). For Arendt's critique of Heidegger, see Dana Villa (1996).

18. Rosalyn Diprose (2010) argues that missing from Arendt's account of what Diprose calls 'a responsive conscience' is a 'consideration of the role of corporeal affectivity or sensibility' (p. 40), for it is the 'immediate shock' Arendt experienced with events following the burning of the Reichstag that Arendt herself identifies as the moment from which, she tells Günter Gaus, 'I felt responsible'. (cited p. 38). To elaborate on what Arendt leaves out, Diprose describes a Nietzschean approach to responsibility that is conditioned by responsiveness based on 'somatic reflexivity' (p. 45). Arendt is suspicious of this kind of materialism as she worries 'the self reduced to biological forces would be the body at the service of totalitarianism, the body that embodies the Law derived...from Nature' (p. 48). However, Diprose, citing Nietzsche, defends it: 'In its reflexivity, the body attempts to enhance pleasure and move beyond pain, but, as pleasure and pain, along with "everything of which we become conscious" are already codified, "interpreted through and through" (*The Will to Power*, p. 477), somatic reflexivity involves contestation and transformation in the meaning of experience, of affects and their relations' (p. 46).

19. Diprose (2010) makes a similar argument when she claims that Arendt criticises 'the conventional juridical concept of self-responsibility, which emphasizes accountability, duty and blame in terms of criteria provided by the prevailing legal and/or moral code. The concept is inadequate insofar as it assumes a self with the *capacity* to act autonomously, to "own" that act, and to know its significance and value in terms of some juridico-moral code' (p. 41). Although Diprose does not go as far as I do with regard to the pluralisation of the legal person, she does observe that the conventional juridical concept of self-responsibility that she identifies with accountability, 'assumes that the self is already temporalized, can remember past acts, anticipate (or promise) future acts, and lives an unbroken continuity from past to future' (p. 41).

20. In *Just Silences*, Marianne Constable (2005) explains why modern law is deaf to the silence of the ones who walk away. 'Modern law and sociology both take language to be social and to be a tool or resource of potentially strategic power. Articulating themselves through language, modern law and sociology leave little room for the nonsocial, for nonpower, for noninstrumentality, be it that of law or language' (p. 176). Constable also suggests that silence may be 'an appropriate response' (p. 174). For instance, she notes that silence may 'point to a legal subject's judgment as to the propriety of conditions of speech in the legal system' (p. 174). What is more, silence may speak in its own way 'of possibilities of justice and injustice in law and language' (p. 174).

REFERENCES

Arendt, H. (1958). *The human condition*. Chicago, IL: University of Chicago Press.

Arendt, H. (1964). *Eichmann in Jerusalem: A report on the banality of evil*. London: Penguin.

Arendt, H. (1965). *On revolution*. London: Penguin.

Arendt, H. (1978a). *The life of the mind. Volume one: Thinking*. New York, NY: Harcourt Brace Jovanovich.

Arendt, H. (1978b). *The life of the mind. Volume two: Willing*. New York, NY: Harcourt Brace Jovanovich.

Arendt, H. (2003a). Personal responsibility under dictatorship. In J. Kohn (Ed.), *Responsibility and judgment* (pp. 17–48). New York, NY: Schocken (Original work published 1964).

Arendt, H. (2003b). Some questions of moral philosophy. In J. Kohn (Ed.), *Responsibility and judgment* (pp. 49–146). New York, NY: Schocken. (Original work published 1965–1966).

Arendt, H. (2003c). Thinking and moral considerations. In J. Kohn (Ed.), *Responsibility and judgment* (pp. 159–189). New York, NY: Schocken (Original work published 1971).

Arendt, H. (2006). Truth and politics. In *Between past and future* (pp. 223–259). London: Penguin.

Bennett, J. (2020). *Influx and efflux: Writing up with Walt Whitman*. Durham, NC: Duke University Press.

Berkowitz, R., Katz, J., & Keenan, T. (Eds.). (2010). *Thinking in dark times: Hannah Arendt on ethics and politics*. New York, NY: Fordham University Press.

Bernstein, R. (2000). Arendt on thinking. In D. Villa (Ed.), *The Cambridge companion to Hannah Arendt* (pp. 277–292). Cambridge: Cambridge University Press.

Constable, M. (2005). *Just silences: The limits and possibilities of modern law*. Princeton, NJ: Princeton University Press.

Constable, M. (2014). *Our word is our bond: How legal speech acts*. Palo Alto, CA: Stanford University Press.

Diprose, R. (2010). Arendt on responsibility, sensibility and democratic pluralism. In A. Schaap, D. Celermajer, & V. Karalis (Eds.), *Power, judgment and political evil* (pp. 39–53). Surrey: Ashgate.

Formasa, P. (2010). Thinking, conscience and acting in times of crises. In A. Schaap, D. Celermajer, & V. Karalis (Eds.), *Power, judgment and political evil* (pp. 89–103). Surrey: Ashgate.

Fuller, L. (1930–1931). Legal fictions. *Illinois Law Review*, *25*(4), 363–399.

Honig, B. (1993). *Political theory and the displacement of politics*. Ithaca, NY: Cornell University Press.

Honig, B. (2017). *Public things: Democracy in disrepair*. New York, NY: Fordham University Press.

Kirkpatrick, J. (2017). *The virtues of exit: On resistance and quitting politics*. Chapel Hill, NC: University of North Carolina Press.

Kohn, J. (2000). Evil and plurality: Hannah Arendt's way to *The Life of the Mind, I*. In L. May & J. Kohn (Eds.), *Hannah Arendt: Twenty years later* (pp. 147–178). Cambridge, MA: MIT Press.

Le Guin, U. (1991). The ones who walk away from Omelas (Variations on a theme by William James). *Utopian Studies*, *2*(1–2), 1–5.

Mahony, D. (2018). *Hannah Arendt's ethics*. London: Bloomsbury Academic.

Massey, H. (2011). When are we when we think? Arendt's temporal interpretation of thinking and thoughtlessness. *Philosophical Topics*, *39*(2), 71–90.

McCleskey v. *Kemp*, 481 U.S. 279 (1987).

Mohamed, S., & Murray, M. (2017). Walking away: Lessons from "Omelas." In A. LaCroix, R. McAdams, & M. Nussbaum (Eds.), *Fatal fictions: Crime and investigation in law and literature* (pp. 227–238). Oxford: Oxford University Press.

Naffine, N. (2003). Who are law's persons? From Cheshire cats to responsible subjects. *The Modern Law Review*, *66*(3), 346–367.

Nietzsche, F. (1990). *Twilight of the idols and the antichrist* (R. J. Hollingdale, Trans.). London: Penguin. (Original work published 1889).

Notes. (2001). What we talk about when we talk about persons: The language of a legal fiction. *Harvard Law Review*, *114*, 1745–1768.

Rothberg, M. (2019). *The implicated subject: Beyond victims and perpetrators*. Palo Alto, CA: Stanford University Press.

Satkunanandan, S. (2015). *Extraordinary responsibility: Politics beyond the moral calculus*. Cambridge: Cambridge University Press.

Schaap, A., Celermajer, D., & Karalis, V. (Eds.). (2010). *Power, judgment and political evil*. Surrey: Ashgate.

Villa, D. (1996). The banality of philosophy: Arendt on Heidegger and Eichmann. In L. May & J. Kohn (Eds.), *Hannah Arendt: Twenty years later* (pp. 179–196). Cambridge, MA: MIT Press.

Whitman, W. (1892). Song of myself. In *Leaves of grass (final "Death-Bed" edition, 1891–2)*. Retrieved from https://www.poetryfoundation.org/poems/45477/song-of-myself-1892-version

CHAPTER 5

THE ROLE OF THE PERSON IN MODERN CONSTITUTIONAL LAW: HOW STATE-INFLICTED HARMS BECOME PERSONAL

Richard Mailey

ABSTRACT

This chapter examines the role of the person in modern constitutional law. Through a reading of two Canadian Supreme Court decisions – RWDSU *v.* Dolphin Delivery *and* R. *v.* Malmo-Levine *– it suggests that while the person is the subject of modern constitutional law's protective gaze, it can also sometimes function as a scapegoat, taking the fall for harms engineered in part by the state (harms, in other words, that really ought to attract constitutional scrutiny given constitutional law's orienting preoccupation with 'state action'). Rather than dismissing these gestures as a result of defective legal reasoning in the cases examined, the chapter suggests that the selective erasure or forgetting of state action is in fact essential to the production of the suffering subject – the constitutional person – that modern constitutional law is supposed to protect, precisely, from the state. In effect, then, the chapter claims that modern constitutional law produces the person by ignoring or at least downplaying the role of the state in certain contexts and, hence, by reneging intermittently on its primary task: the application of legal scrutiny to coercive state action.*

Keywords: The person; constitutional personhood; *Canadian Charter of Rights and Freedoms*; state action doctrine; criminalisation; constitutional theory

Interrupting the Legal Person
Studies in Law, Politics, and Society, Volume 87A, 73–88

ISSN: 1059-4337/doi:10.1108/S1059-43372022000087A005

INTRODUCTION

What role does the concept of 'the person' play in modern constitutional law? A standard answer to this question might assume that contemporary constitutionalism is defined by its framing of the person as a bearer of an inalienable dignity which denotes the limits of legitimate state action. (McCrudden, 2008). Of course, this is undeniably a core symbolic and practical role that the person plays in modern constitutions and constitutional jurisprudence. But it is not the only one. On the contrary, while invocations of personhood offer an important means of holding the modern state to account, they can also let the state escape such accountability by offering up a fall guy or scapegoat that can take the blame for contra-constitutional harm (i.e. harm that violates or offends constitutional values but that is not necessarily unconstitutional, legally speaking) in which the state is in fact deeply imbricated. In making this argument, the present chapter aims to explicate and grapple with a paradox that has been highlighted by a number of other scholars (e.g. Veitch, 2007; Williams, 2007) and that is summed up by observing, with Veitch, that modern constitutional and human rights law often seems to fall silent when it is in theory most applicable, in the face of grand, highly coordinated schemes of human suffering (Veitch, 2007). The question is: what role might judicial framings of personhood play in the legitimation of such suffering, and in the production of the seemingly counter-intuitive state of affairs whereby constitutional law sometimes seems to withdraw its interest entirely from the phenomenon that generally appears as its core concern, that is, *human suffering* (see Williams, 2007)?

Rather than addressing this question in purely abstract terms, the chapter will examine a number of concrete examples – as per the methodology of Pavlich (2007), as well as Pavlich's chapter in this collection (2022) which itself relies on Agamben (2009) – of the way that judicial constructions of personhood divert attention from and selectively erase state violence in constitutional law, even as they provide an often effective language for holding perpetrators of such violence to account. The point of this examination, to be clear, is not to suggest that all modern constitutional systems treat the figure of the treat the person in exactly the same way, although certain systems may indeed overlap. Rather, the point is to use a number of 'paradigmatic' (see Agamben, 2009) examples of judicial argumentation to spotlight a fundamental problem at the heart of many and perhaps most modern systems of constitutional law: the problem of how constitutional law's apparently *exclusive* concern with 'state action' and state-inflicted harm – as opposed to the actions of private legal persons – can be maintained when the state plays such a key role in contouring and violently protecting spheres of purportedly private action; spheres supposedly inhabited, at least predominantly, by private legal persons making private, free choices for themselves.

To be more precise, the chapter will hone-in on two examples drawn from the Supreme Court of Canada's (or the 'SCC's') jurisprudence on the *Canadian Charter of Rights and Freedoms* (1982), a fully constitutional bill of rights that is often presented as a particularly laudable embodiment of democratic values (Albert, 2017), including the notion value of human dignity mentioned above

(Weinrib, 2004). To begin with, sections one and two will examine the SCC's controversial *RWDSU* v. *Dolphin Delivery* (1986) decision, its first word on the extent to which the *Charter* applies to private as well as state action. Then, in section three, the chapter will turn briefly to an arguably more glaring instance of the person-as-scapegoat operation in the SCC's *R.* v. *Malmo-Levine* (2003) judgement, which considered but ultimately minimised the Canadian state's constitutional responsibility for the harms of criminalisation. Put simply, what these two decisions show is how a judicial assumption of a pure, 'unencumbered' (Sandel, 1984) sphere of private personhood beyond (and with little or no major dependence on) the state can take the heat off the state for its role in the creation of contra-constitutional harm. In both cases, the relevant violations would not have been experienced without an organised network of deliberate state choices. And yet, by a fascinating sleight of hand, the SCC regards the relevant harms in each case as products of *personal* choices that the state merely honours. In the end, my tentative suggestion is that far from being momentary, correctible defects in judicial reasoning, these moments of 'responsibility transference' (Veitch, 2007, p. 60) shed light on a contradiction that lies at the heart of liberal-democratic constitutionalism (or rather, a paradigm thereof) as a form of political order that simultaneously recognises and disavows its role in the production of social reality (see Singer, 2012, for an example of this argument). With all of this in mind, we can proceed now to the chapter's first section, which examines the SCC's *Dolphin Delivery* judgement, below.

DOLPHIN DELIVERY: THE LEGAL DENIAL OF POLITICAL SCIENCE?

Following in the footsteps of the Americans to the South, the Canadians' *Charter of Rights and Freedoms* (1982) binds state but not private actors (Americans know this requirement as the 'state action doctrine' [see Chemerinsky, 1985]). However, while the *Charter* doesn't apply to and limit the conduct of private legal persons directly, it was initially unclear after its passage if and how it might apply to private persons *indirectly*, by altering private legal rights and hence altering the courses of action that are in fact open to private legal persons and entities. Given the fundamentality of this question – the question of scope, let's call it – to the *Charter's* application, it was surely inevitable that it would quickly find its way before the federal Supreme Court, as it did just four years after the *Charter* was passed in *RWDSU* v. *Dolphin Delivery* (1986). In a nutshell, the *Dolphin* case involved an industrial dispute between a trade union (RWDSU) representing employees of a large courier company (Purolator), and another courier company (Dolphin Delivery) that was allegedly acting as a business ally of Purolator in British Columbia. When RWDSU threatened to picket Dolphin's premises 'to publicize [its] industrial dispute' (Hogg, 1987, p. 273) with Purolator, Dolphin sued for injunctive relief. After an injunction was granted at first instance (on the grounds that the threatened action would constitute tortious 'secondary picketing' [Hogg, 1987, p. 273]), RWDSU appealed, claiming that such secondary picketing, while indeed contrary to the common law, was now protected by the *Charter's* guarantee of free expression (1982, section 2b). Did the *Charter* even apply, though, if it didn't bind private actors like Dolphin? By the time the case reached the Canadian Supreme Court, everything hinged on this question – the question of scope – rather than the substantive question of whether secondary picketing amounted to constitutionally protected expression under the *Charter*. As noted above, the *Charter* didn't and doesn't apply directly to a private legal person like Dolphin; but did it apply to either the common law rules that allowed Dolphin to block the picketing, or to the BC courts that enforced those rules?

On the first front, that is, with respect to the common law, the straightforward argument on RWDSU's side was that the *Constitution Act* (1982) – of which the *Charter* is the first part – makes the *Charter* and the Constitution applicable without exception to all law, specifically when it states that '*any law* [my emphasis]... that is inconsistent with the provisions of the Constitution is, to the extent of the inconsistency, of no force or effect' (section 52). On the latter front, that is, with respect to the courts, the arguably more strained argument is that section 32(1) of the *Constitution Act* makes the *Charter* applicable to Canada's federal and provincial governments (isn't the judiciary clearly an organ of government?). How, then, did the SCC respond to these claims?

Let's start with the second argument, on the applicability of the *Charter* to the courts. In responding to this claim, the SCC essentially makes two counter-arguments: one legalistic, one political. The broadly plausible, legalistic argument was based on the fact that in section 32 of the *Constitution Act* (1982), the *Charter* is not simply made applicable to government, but to 'the Parliament and the government of Canada' and to the legislatures and governments of the various provinces. The only sensible way to understand this clause, the *Dolphin* court suggests, is by reading the term 'government' as a narrow reference to the executive branch on its own. To read it otherwise – and more specifically, to read it as a reference to all three, core branches of government taken together – would seem to produce a clunky tautology, with the provision then making the *Charter* applicable to 'Parliament, *parliament*, the executive and the judiciary' (see *RWDSU* v. *Dolphin Delivery*, 1986, pp. 598–601).

While this may strike one as a very reasonable (although not unassailable) argument, such legalism was apparently not sufficient to shore up the court's position, and Justice MacIntyre's majority opinion accordingly proceeds to back it up with a political argument on why it would be unacceptable to regard the judiciary as a potential party to a constitutional dispute. To quote MacIntyre in full on this:

> I find the ... [suggestion that the judiciary is subject to constitutional scrutiny] ... troublesome and, in my view, it should not be accepted as an approach to this problem. *While in political science terms* ... [my emphasis] it is probably acceptable to treat the courts as one of the three fundamental branches of Government, that is, legislative, executive, and judicial, I cannot equate for the purposes of *Charter* application the order of a court with an element of governmental action. This is not to say that the courts are not bound by the *Charter*. The courts are, of course, bound by the *Charter* as they are bound by all law. It is their duty to apply the law, but in doing

> so they act as *neutral arbiters* ... [my emphasis], not as contending parties involved in a dispute. To regard a court order as an element of governmental intervention necessary to invoke the *Charter* would, it seems to me, widen the scope of *Charter* application to virtually all private litigation. All cases must end, if carried to completion, with an enforcement order and if the *Charter* precludes the making of the order, where a *Charter* right would be infringed, it would seem that all private litigation would be subject to the *Charter*. In my view, this approach will not provide the answer to the question. A more direct and a more precisely-defined connection between the element of government action and the claim advanced must be present before the *Charter* applies. (*RWDSU* v. *Dolphin Delivery*, 1986, pp. 600–601)

Let's take a moment to unpack this. What does MacIntyre mean when he suggests that the judiciary can 'probably' be regarded as an organ of government 'in political science terms'? Without ascribing a definitive intention to MacIntyre here, the simplest connotation that one might draw from this is perhaps the one highlighted by Robert Cover's (1986) famous essay, 'Violence and the Word'. To quote Cover:

> Legal interpretation takes place in a field of pain and death. This is true in several senses. Legal interpretive acts signal and occasion the imposition of violence upon others: A judge articulates her understanding of a text, and as a result, somebody loses his freedom, his property, his children, even his life. Interpretations in law also constitute justifications for violence which has already occurred or which is about to occur. When interpreters have finished their work, they frequently leave behind victims whose lives have been torn apart by these organized, social practices of violence. Neither legal interpretation nor the violence it occasions may be properly understood apart from one another. (Cover, 1986, p. 1601)

From this perspective, then, courts can be regarded as organs of government because their interpretive acts and decisions are 'supported by the full panoply of state power' (*Shelley* v. *Kraemer*, 1948), occasioning precisely the sorts of 'organized, social practices of violence' that one may assume constitutional law is supposed to render legally contestable. While a nod to an article linking law and violence is surely too much to expect from a court of law, a nod to the US Supreme Court (USSC) judgement just quoted, *Shelley* v. *Kramer*, would have been more than appropriate, especially given the interest it had already drawn from Canadian constitutional scholars like Peter Hogg (1985) in his *Constitutional Law of Canada*. In *Shelley*, after years of denial and avoidance, the Supreme Court ruled that a judicial decision to enforce a racially discriminatory agreement between private legal persons constituted state action for constitutional purposes. In taking this approach, the USSC effectively embraced the very same 'political science' perspective that the *Dolphin* court consciously opted to ignore, thereby 'constitutionalising' what Cover would later flag as an obvious but routinely underemphasised feature of judicial enforcement orders: namely, that they occasion a form of 'organized' violence that is hard to distinguish, for those on the receiving end, from the organised practices of violence that flow from an executive order or an act of legislation. Why could the *Dolphin* court not bring itself to make this leap as well, in the footsteps of *Shelley*?

We can leave this question hanging for now as we return to the second argument that the SCC responded to in *Dolphin Delivery*: the argument that the *Charter* applies to common law rules like the one enforced by the BC courts. As noted above, there are strong reasons for supposing that the *Charter* should and does apply indiscriminately to the common law, most notably on account of the Canadian *Constitution Act's* (1982, section 52) unqualified insistence that unconstitutionality will invalidate 'any law'. However, what the *Constitution Act* doesn't specify is whether constitutional law will apply to all law *in exactly the same way*, and it is in the context of this interpretive gap that Justice MacIntyre proceeds to distinguish, in *Dolphin*, between the *Charter's* impact on private and public disputes. To explain this distinction, then: where the state is a party in a legal dispute, MacIntyre suggests that the common law rules that are at stake will be subject to normal constitutional scrutiny, which is to say that, if they are found to violate *Charter* rights, they must be justified by the state in accordance with the SCC's relatively taxing proportionality test (derived from section 1 of the *Charter*). By contrast, where a legal dispute is exclusively between private parties, an aggrieved individual can no longer claim that enforcement of a common law rule would violate their *Charter* rights, but only that the courts should 'apply and develop' the common law in a 'manner consistent with the fundamental values enshrined in the Constitution' (*RWDSU* v. *Dolphin Delivery*, 1986, p. 603), and that this requires a decision in their favour. As the SCC later clarified in *Hill* v. *Church of Scientology* (1995), the consequential differences between these two forms of *Charter* application are that the latter option (1) involves a weaker 'balancing test' that is more likely to lead to the maintenance of the legal status quo, and (2) places the burden of proof on the aggrieved individual rather than the state (also increasing the chances of a decision for the status quo).

Curiously, while this constitutional distinction between public and private law applies to the common law, MacIntyre is explicit in noting that it doesn't apply to private law legislation. Once again, then, there is an awkward separation at issue between judicial and legislative power, a distinction that is apparently blind to the way that both forms of power involve an organised infliction of violence that will be indistinguishable at the critical point of its reception. Here, though, there is no legalistic justification for the distinction (as there arguably was with section 32's 'Parliament and government' clause), and, to make things worse, it produces a nonsensical state of affairs in which a statute codifying a common law rule could be invalidated only to leave the common law rule itself fully in force and immune from full-fledged *Charter* review (although subject to the 'balancing' test mentioned above). Given this lack of legal grounding *and* practical value, how, one wonders, do we explain the court's decision to insulate the common law rules applicable to private persons from *full* constitutional scrutiny? Isn't an odd amount of effort required to sustain this position, and to suppress the political science 'truth' affirmed in *Shelley* and noted, if only in passing, by Justice MacIntyre; the truth that private action, the action of private legal persons, relies heavily on 'organized, social practices of violence' (Cover, 1986, p. 1601) in which the state plays the pivotal role?

HUTCHINSON AND PETTER ON THE 'LIBERAL LIE OF THE CHARTER'

Two years after the *Dolphin* case was decided, Alan Hutchinson and Andrew Petter (1988) (HP hereafter) wrote a potent critique of the ruling that can help us to decipher these puzzles. Turning to this critique now, the first question that presents itself, and that takes us immediately to the heart of HP's argument, is on the subtitle that they used for their article: 'The Liberal Lie of the Charter'. What could HP have meant by this? The initial inference that one may draw is that HP aren't *necessarily* accusing the *Dolphin* court and Justice MacIntyre of poor legal reasoning. On the contrary, if we take the subtitle at its word, HP's target actually appears to be the *Charter* itself, not (or not just) Justice MacIntyre and his judicial colleagues. As HP (1988) explain, confirming this inference:

> Although it is tempting to write off [*Dolphin's*] … internal contradiction as evidence of a confused and incompetent judiciary, such an assessment is both too harsh and too kind. It is too harsh because the contradiction is not one of the court's own making; it is a reflection of the inherent contradiction of liberal ideology in a positivist age. It is too kind because the political implications of the contradiction are more pervasive and pernicious than if it had been a product of mere confusion or incompetence. (p. 283)

What do HP mean, though, when they refer to the 'inherent contradiction of liberal ideology in a positive age'? To understand this claim, we first need to understand the decidedly non-positivist, natural law perspective that anchored previously dominant versions of North American liberalism (Chemerinsky, 1985, pp. 511–513; Ely, 1980, p. 48). Without oversimplifying, one may say that this perspective encompasses three key ideas. Firstly, it encompasses the idea that individual rights are not a product of human action (as legal positivists would have it), but are simply and naturally there, waiting to be recognised (hence why it's a 'natural law' perspective). Secondly, it encompasses the Blackstonian belief that there is no meaningful distance between the principles of the English and later North American common law and the principles of natural law (Chemerinsky, 1985, p. 512; Cover, 1975, p. 15; Kennedy, 1978, p. 241). And thirdly, it presupposes a hierarchy of laws whereby (1) core common law principles are superior to statute law (on what grounds could a legislature legitimately override natural rights?), and (2) the common law is coincident with constitutional law (as Chemerinsky explains, the US Bill of Rights was originally seen as granting explicit recognition to the natural rights of individuals against the state in the same way that the common law was seen as protecting their natural rights against one another [Chemerinsky, 1985, pp. 511–514]).

While HP certainly aren't fans of this archaic, natural law perspective, they claim that the problems that it faces are in some ways 'less daunting' (p. 284) than the contradictoriness that the *Dolphin* court embroils itself in by seemingly pairing the Blackstonian sanctification of the common law – without explanation, one may add – with a more positivist perspective (a perspective that is evident, for example, in Justice MacIntyre's concession that courts may well be regarded as state actors in 'political science' terms). To begin explaining this point, consider the simplest truth that one buys into by swapping a natural law theory for a positivist one: namely, that all law, including the common law, is a contingent product of human action (i.e. as positive or posited law). The problem is that when one accepts this seemingly simple truth (as the *Dolphin* court seems to [see HP, 1988, p. 291]), one opens a very big can of worms with respect to the public–private distinction and the state action doctrine, because if all law is posited, state law, then the state is implicated in all private affairs insofar as those affairs are contoured by rules and standards that it has freely chosen (not rules and standards that are simply and immutably 'there'). In this sense, as Peller and Tushnet put it, 'state regulation of *so-called private conduct*… [my emphasis] is always present, as a matter of analytic necessity, within a legal order' (Peller & Tushnet, 2003, p. 789; see also Singer & Saidel-Goley, 2018; Sunstein, 2002; Van der Walt, 2014). To quote Jacques Derrida (1997), one may accordingly say that a positivist perspective leaves 'nothing outside the text' (p. 163) of the state and its law; no antecedent order that enables one to distinguish between purely facilitative state action (state action that simply protects natural rights and liberties) and the intrusive, discretionary state action that is subject to constitutional scrutiny.

Crucially, although HP point to the *Dolphin* court's explicit acceptance of positivist premises, their argument doesn't *need* to show this. On the contrary, even if the court showed no direct acknowledgement of the simple truth that all law is posited or positive law, one may *infer* its at least partial, inconsistent acceptance of this truth from the fact that, insofar as it includes a formula for its own democratic amendment, the Canadian *Constitution Act* (1982) presents itself not as the codification of immutable, natural truths, but as an eminently provisional, incomplete decision by the Canadian people (or peoples) to '*hold* certain truths to be self-evident' for the time being (on the difference between these two perspectives, see Arendt, 2006, p. 185; Van der Walt, 2012, p. 80). In this sense, the contradiction at stake here – the 'liberal lie' of the *Charter* as HP call it – is not specific to the Canadian system, or even to what HP call the 'post-realist age' in North America (see HP, 1988, pp. 290–291). Rather, the liberal lie of the *Charter* is the lie of a particular paradigm of *liberal democratic constitutionalism*, the lie of a system that simultaneously presents constitutional identity as an ultimately 'empty space' (see Lefort, 2006, pp. 160–161), potentially subject to an ongoing, democratic process of redefinition, and as a status bounded by actually self-evident liberties – liberties, in other words, that precede and constrain the activity of all positive, democratic lawmaking, including constitutional lawmaking.

Put simply, then, if a state presents itself as democratic all the way down – that is, if it endorses the idea that the will of the people is the transcendent source of all law, including constitutional law – then it is also presenting itself as positivist all the way down, thereby undermining the public–private distinction insofar as a positivist perspective implicates the state in all private affairs as the author and enforcer of the rules that contour those affairs (as per Hale and Hohfeld [see Peller & Tushnet, 2003, p. 789]). However, while clinging to the public–private distinction by proceeding 'as if' (see Motha, 2018 on 'as if' moments in law) certain state actors are not really acting falsely denies the inherent positivism of the Canadian Constitution, dispensing with the public–private distinction is problematic for the very same reason: namely, because it casts aside a clearly stated part of the *Charter*, the state action rule derived, in part, from the Constitution's 'Parliament and government' clause. In this sense, as HP note, the *Charter* can be seen as a cocktail of contradictory premises and, indeed, contradictory conceptions of sovereignty; one that accepts the undivided sovereignty of the state (or the Canadian people), and another that draws a line between that sovereignty and the 'pre-political' (HP, 1988, p. 284) sovereignty of the person (a person whose liberties, powers and choices owe nothing, originally, to the state and its law). *This* is why HP stress that they aren't criticising the *Dolphin* court, as such; because the *Dolphin* court was in their words 'between a rock and a hard place' (HP, 1988, p. 290), doomed to the enforcement of a philosophically confused constitutional code.

With this confusion in mind, let's steer the ship back to our main question, though: the question of how the person functions in modern constitutional law. As we can now see, my initial formulation of the contradiction whereby a body of law designed to protect the person ends up deploying the person as a scapegoat to thwart the law's protective function (or whereby the constitutional quest for state accountability is marked as paramount at the same time as potentially problematic state action is recast as constitutionally irrelevant private action) is complex. To explain this complexity, one may say that if the line between the public and the private is illusory, and is effectively produced by judicial decision-making, then the realm of the personal – the private realm of the private person – is not simply 'used' as a scapegoat for state violence, but is actually *produced* by writing the state out of the story in certain situations. In *Dolphin*, the denial that certain common law rules constitute *fully* actionable state action produces a pure(-ish) personal relation that otherwise doesn't exist or, more precisely, exists only in law (not outside the text of the law, per Derrida). Having created this personal relation, the attribution of responsibility for harm becomes a private law question rather than a constitutional law one, since private persons are the only actors on stage. This is why I am describing the legal person as a scapegoat for state violence in constitutional law; because the appearance of the socially extracted legal person on the scene obscures the state's role in actually permitting, facilitating and enforcing destructive states of affairs and, more specifically, contra-constitutional states of affairs – states of affairs that are out of step with constitutional norms but are not *technically* unconstitutional in a strict, legal sense (often because of rules like the state action doctrine).

Although this is a deeply problematic move, it stems from a contradiction of liberal–democratic constitutionalism that is 'inevitable' (Christodoulidis, 2009, p. 6) in the sense that it 'can neither be displaced nor ignored' (Christodoulidis, 2009, p. 6) without an abrupt reorientation of public values (a reorientation that moves away from the constitutional paradigm just described). As noted above with reference to HP's article, the contradiction is that liberal–democratic constitutions often commit, simultaneously, to two visions of sovereignty; one that posits self-evident truths that no sovereignty can touch or change, and one that views sovereignty as the creative force behind all law, and that therefore regards even the fundamental liberties of the person as contingent products of political power at a given point in time. To maintain a semblance of balance between these two, opposing visions, courts in cases like *Dolphin* have little choice but to choose between the deployment of legal fictions that maintain the public–private distinction – *the* fundamental distinction of the first vision of sovereignty, one might say – and the recognition of 'political science' truths that undermine that distinction, but that promote the full accountability of the state for its contra-constitutional conduct. In the face of this choice, could MacIntyre and his colleagues have produced anything other than an opinion seemingly at odds with itself?

MALMO-LEVINE: CRIMINALISATION AS A SELF-INFLICTED WOUND

To sum this up, then, in *Dolphin Delivery* state-made and enforced restrictions on free speech are converted into predominantly interpersonal restrictions beyond the scope of constitutional law's exclusive concern with state action; restrictions whereby a private person (as opposed to the state) limits the speech of another private person. There may be a personal violation or harm at stake in these restrictions, but the court's curt denial of fully actionable state action prevents that violation or harm from registering, meaningfully and consequentially, as a relevant concern of Canada's state-centric constitutional law. In this regard, as Williams (2007) puts it in relation to human rights law generally, Canada's jurisprudence on the *Charter's* state action rule turns on a logic of 'sufferance' rather than 'insufferability' (pp. 13–20). The SCC recognises suffering, but refuses to mark it as *insufferable*, that is, as a constitutionally significant phenomenon that 'demands [remedial or injunctive] action as a consequence' (Williams, 2007, p. 13).

Shifting gears now, this section will move from this interpersonal recasting of state violence to a second, arguably more glaring version of the same operation. With this second example, the SCC's *R.* v. *Malmo-Levine* (2003) decision, an even more expansive, palpable and engulfing web of state violence – the life-changing violence of criminalisation – is re-spun in passing to produce an act not of interpersonal harm, but of individual *self-harm*. While *R.* v. *Malmo-Levine* (2003) is surely best known for its detailed consideration of whether a Millian 'harm principle' is part of Canada's post-*Charter* constitutional law (see pp. 630–640), the focus of this section will be confined to a sequence of short passages in which the court addresses and ultimately minimises the Canadian state's responsibility for harms stemming from criminalisation. To put these sections in context, suffice it to say that *Malmo-Levine* involved a pair of claims brought by individuals convicted of marijuana possession, one by an individual (Malmo-Levine) who ran a club instructing marijuana users on 'safe smoking habits' (*R.* v. *Malmo-Levine*, 2003, p. 592), and one by an individual (Caine) who was caught smoking pot in his car by passing police officers. While the claimants conceded that marijuana use is associated with 'harmful effects' (*R.* v. *Malmo-Levine*, 2003, p. 592), they argued, *inter alia,* that criminalisation – and in particular, criminalisation with the possibility of imprisonment – was a disproportionate and hence unconstitutional way of attempting to reduce these harmful effects; a strategy that caused substantially more harm than it prevented. To put this in more technical, legal–constitutional terms, the question before the SCC (or at least one of the main questions) was whether the criminalisation of marijuana possession violated section 7 of the *Charter* (1982), which forbids state deprivations of 'life, liberty and security of the person' that are not 'in accordance with the principles of fundamental justice', including a principle of 'gross disproportionality' (Hogg, 2012, p. 204) requiring (1) that the deprivation is in pursuit of a 'legitimate state interest' (Hogg, 2012, p. 204), and (2) that it is 'not grossly disproportionate to [that] … state interest' (Hogg, 2012, p. 204).

Before the court addressed this question of 'gross disproportionality', it hinted at the perspective it would take when it dismissed the idea that the state's criminalisation of marijuana possession causes users to experience 'serious psychological distress' (see *R.* v. *Morgentaler*, 1988) in a way that potentially violates section 7's security of the person provision. In dismissing this argument, the court argued that since marijuana was accepted – including by the claimants – to be 'non-addictive' (*R.* v. *Malmo-Levine*, 2003, p. 624), any psychological distress experienced by users worried about the risk of prosecution could be avoided by a simple, free choice to stop using. When the court then came to deal with the gross proportionality principle some pages later in its decision, one finds much the same logic at work, with the state-inflicted harm of criminalisation reduced to a matter of individually chosen self-harm. In particular, one can see this logic clearly when the court notes that the various direct and 'collateral consequences' (see Hoskins, 2018) of criminalisation ('not least among them the possibility of a criminal record' [*R.* v. *Malmo-Levine*, 2003, p. 653]), as 'deleterious' (*R.* v. *Malmo-Levine*, 2003, p. 654) as they may be, 'are *largely* the product of *deliberate* disobedience to the law of land [my emphases]' (*R.* v. *Malmo-Levine*, 2003, p. 655). As the court continues:

> [If a] … court imposes a sentence on conviction that is no more than a fit sentence, which it is required to do, the other adverse consequences are really associated with the criminal justice system in general rather than this offence in particular. In any system of criminal law there will be prosecutions that turn out to be unfounded, publicity that is unfairly adverse, costs associated with a successful defense, lingering and perhaps unfair consequences attached to a conviction for a relatively minor offence by other jurisdictions, and so on. These effects are serious but they are part of the social and individual costs of having a criminal justice system. Whenever Parliament exercises its criminal law power, such costs will arise. To suggest that such 'inherent' costs are fatal to the exercise of the power is to overshoot the function of s. 7. (*R.* v. *Malmo-Levine*, 2003, p. 656)

At first blush, the court's point in this passage might seem to be that because the Constitution grants criminal lawmaking power to Canada's federal parliament, it can generally be presumed that the normal exercise of this power (and the production of consequences that ordinarily follow on from it, however severe) is legitimate and constitutional. Of course, if this is what the court means, then it is on shaky ground, because modern constitutions grant a great many powers to state actors that are nonetheless very broadly subject to judicial review and scrutiny. Indeed, *this* is the whole point of the *Charter*; to provide a new, *dignitarian* legal language in which otherwise valid exercises of state power that produce personal or social harm and indignity can be legally challenged, with the state called on to defend its choices in open court (see *R.* v. *Malmo-Levine*, 2003, pp. 673–674 [Justice Arbour Dissent]). When one recalls this fundamental, decisive function of the *Charter*, does it not start to seem strange that the court would embrace such an apparently broad presumption that harm flowing from exercises of the state's criminal law power is constitutionally tolerable?

The court's moralistic suggestion that these harms flow from 'deliberate disobedience of the law of the land' perhaps explains and quells this strangeness. With these words, the court seems to be endorsing a conception of personal responsibility that requires (at least) three things: that an infraction has been committed, that the author knows the rule, and finally that he is in control of his acts to the point of having been able to act differently (Ricoeur, 2000, p. 24)

The court is not, then, engaged in a narrow line of argumentation over whether a constitutional conferral of official power necessarily implies constitutional tolerance of all the 'normal' consequences of its exercise. Rather, there seems to be something important for the court, and critically so, in the *intent* of the criminalised person. They, *the person*, must shoulder the various consequences of criminalisation not just because these consequences are a 'normal' product of the constitutional system, but also because they, the person, have *chosen* them. Never mind that they have 'chosen' them from a scant menu (see Veitch, 2007, pp. 52–59), that this menu was a creation of the state (Canada's federal parliament), and that fulfilment of their 'order' would have depended on a further array of state choices (police, prosecutorial, judicial, etc.) to pursue and realise their rebirth as a criminal subject. Forget all of that; the criminalised person had access to the menu, and they ordered. Didn't they know, as a presumably free and rational person, what they were ordering?

Of course, sometimes the law accepts a negative answer to this question, including where it appears that a defendant couldn't have known what they were ordering, or where the law afforded them only a tragic choice between catastrophic alternatives. In such cases – for example, in cases of strict liability crimes (see the *BC Motor Vehicle* [1985] case), or where obedience of the law would itself yield serious harm (as in *Bedford* v. *Attorney General* [2013] on the state's responsibility for harms linked to its criminal regulation of sex work) –the SCC has indeed been willing to articulate and pin down limits on the federal parliament's criminal law power. However, far from tempering the fictive, individualising logic of *Malmo-Levine*, these cases confirm it by making *everything* turn on the question of individual responsibility. In effect, the idea that we're left with is that the state only enters the picture as a coercive force (and only *acts*) when it goes beyond enforcing a construction of the individual's rational will, a construction that is produced by asking whether a rational person in the individual's position would have chosen to break the law. Where the law asks the individual to refrain from doing something that is deemed unimportant in law, like smoking pot in *Malmo-Levine*, the flat assumption is that a normal, rational person would tolerate its full application – even to themselves – to attain the package of 'inestimable benefits' (Michelman, 2003) of an effective system of criminal law (see again the quoted passages from *R.* v. *Malmo-Levine*, 2003 p. 656). By contrast, when the law asks the individual to do something impossible or to refrain from doing something that the law deems critically important, like exercising a fundamental right, the previous presumption is rebutted (as in cases like *Bedford*). In both cases, the role of the state is simply to honour and enforce individual choice; everything that happens next can be traced back to that choice and attributed to that chooser, not to the various state choices that are required to frame that choice and, indeed, to define the legal person as a rational, responsible chooser.

In effect, this is where the enterprise of the *Charter* – and the paradigm of liberal–democratic constitutionalism that it embodies – shows itself to be a double-edged sword. On the one hand, the phenomenal achievement of modern bills of rights like the *Charter*, as McCrudden (2008) notes, is that they have symbolically subordinated the state to the individual, safeguarding each individual's basic interest in the free development of their own personality (with varying degrees of success, of course). On the other hand, and contrary to complaints that the language of human rights negates the recognition of individual responsibilities, defining the individual in terms of their agency, and their capacity for free choice, feeds into a sense that they *and they alone* are responsible for their fates, with the state's role in contouring and violently enforcing what eventually look like individual choices receding deep into the sub-constitutional background. Without the presence of the state in *Malmo-Levine* – without a whole gamut of state choices that are required to bring an instance of criminalisation to fruition – things look radically different for the original claimants. There is a real element of personal choice in their marijuana use, and their violation of criminal law, of course; but it is far from the only or even the main choice that is required to produce their criminalisation and its many damaging and potentially life-spanning consequences.

With this point in mind, one can perhaps now more clearly understand the paradox of legal personhood that this chapter seeks to unpack. To summarise my argument, then, suffice it to say again that the person that modern constitutional law aims to protect is produced by denying (at least some of) the institutional forces and decisions that are required to bring it to appearance, including certain state decisions that regard and indeed constitute that person as a broadly rational, responsible subject, *the* subject with which modern constitutional law is concerned insofar as it is about protecting certain purportedly paramount moments of individual liberty and choice. The rub is that for this subject or person to appear, it is accordingly necessary to deny exactly that which constitutional law is supposed to protect it against: namely, the full expanse of state sovereignty. Where the constitutive sovereign decision is denied, the person – the private legal person as a free, rational decision-maker, non-reliant on the state – comes to appearance, but what is left to protect that person against when this decision is denied? Only, I would aver, those decisions that violate the person as constituted by the state; not those in some senses more fundamental decisions that actually *make* persons in specific, contestable ways, and that produce necessarily unnatural schemes of suffering and inequality as a matter of course.

CONCLUSION: BETWEEN TWO SYSTEMS

To conclude now, let's return to the reference to Andrew Williams with which the last section began. Human rights law, Williams (2007) says, promises to address suffering, but it does so through a logic of 'sufferance' rather than 'insufferability' (pp. 13–19), with most instances of judicially recognised human suffering marked as excusable, tolerable or legally irrelevant (a cursory glance at the stats shows that the majority of human rights claims are indeed met with this conclusion). However, even if an effort was made to make human rights law more robust as a response to human suffering, it would still have a baked-in blind spot insofar as it is premised on the production of a singular suffering subject, a subject that can only be produced by obscuring the role of the state – and indeed, a range of other social forces a range of other social forces – in bringing this subject to appearance as a person with a certain range of powers and capacities and liberties and choices. Without this denial of the role that state decisions play in the production of legal persons, there is no independent, singular, suffering subject, but the denial of these decisions also, paradoxically, insulates the state from precisely the type of legal accountability that is supposed to ensure the protection of that same suffering subject. To be held to account at all, in other words, the state must disappear certain parts of itself in order to produce a figure, *a person*, to be shielded from those other parts of itself (those sovereign *choices*) that it can tolerate exposing to the cold light of constitutional scrutiny.

To be clear, this is not to say that a particular image of the legal person emerges suddenly with the fictional eradication of the state in decisions like *Dolphin Delivery* and *Malmo-Levine*. On the contrary, what happens in both of these cases is that the SCC chooses to insulate an old, pre-*Charter* conception of the legal person against the uncertain and potentially revolutionary forces of the *Charter* (although constitutional review is 'revolutionary' in a very limited sense). In this regard, Peter Hogg (1987) doesn't go quite far enough when he describes the *Dolphin* decision as an 'imperfect knitting together' (p. 279) of contradictory opinions. In actuality, as HP point out, it is the *Charter* that is itself an imperfect knitting together of contradictory *systems* – an old system of more or less stable legal categories, and a new system in which all such categories must somehow be squared with a new set of purportedly 'supreme' legal values (a set of values that are *themselves* at odds in certain ways). As Williams (2007) suggests, these two systems *can* coexist, but only where relevant actors assume, as the SCC seems to, that the old system has no *intrinsic* social cost from the perspective of the new system (see Williams, 2007, pp. 15–16). Where this assumption persists, judicial 'synthesis' (see Ackerman, 1993, pp. 131–162) of the two systems is achievable, with the *Charter's* system of justiciable constitutional rights mopping up occasional, isolated instances of state abuse while leaving the old system – its basic categories and its distribution of rights and entitlements – fully intact and operational. However, when one accepts that the system itself is comprised of a whole 'panoply' (*Shelley* v. *Kraemer*, 1948) of state choices about when to prevent, tolerate or engineer suffering, synthesis becomes implausible, and constitutional judges face a stark choice between the deployment of fictions that shield core parts of the old system from scrutiny, and the exposure of the system in its entirety (including highly political, 'allocative' decisions) to the unpredictable, gusty winds of (judicial) re-evaluation. The question that we must leave hanging is whether there is a way of tempering these gusty winds without leaning on the counter-productive fiction that the state, *the sovereign*, is sometimes absent in its own territory (on this see Van der Walt, 2014). Can we embrace the relentless exposure and mitigation of sovereign violence – and the full responsibility of the sovereign for its own territory – without also embracing a strong sense of 'juristocracy' (Hirschl, 2007), the effectively sovereign rule of the judges charged with this relentless task?

REFERENCES

Ackerman, B. (1993). *We the people, volume I: Foundations*. Cambridge, MA: Harvard University Press.

Agamben, G. (2009). *The signature of all things: On method*. New York, NY: Zone Books.

Albert, R. (2017). Introduction: The values of Canadian constitutionalism. In R. Albert & D. R. Cameron (Eds.), *Canada in the world: Comparative perspectives on the Canadian constitution* (pp. 1–24). Cambridge: Cambridge University Press.

Arendt, H. (2006). *On revolution*. London: Penguin.

Canada (Attorney General) v. *Bedford* [2013] 3 S.C.R. 1101.

Canadian Charter of Rights and Freedoms, Part 1 of the *Constitution Act*, 1982, being Schedule B to the Canada Act 1982 (UK), 1982, c 11.

Chemerinsky, E. (1985). Rethinking state action. *Northwestern University Law Review*, *80*(3), 503–557.

Christodoulidis, E. (2009). Strategies of rupture. *Law and Critique*, *20*, 3–26.

Cover, R. M. (1975). *Justice accused: Antislavery and the judicial process*. New Haven, CT: Yale University Press.

Cover, R. M. (1986). Violence and the word. *The Yale Law Journal*, *95*(8), 1601–1629.

Derrida, J. (1997). *Of grammatology* (G. C. Spivak, Trans.). Baltimore, MD: Johns Hopkins University Press.

Ely, J. H. (1980). *Democracy and distrust: A theory of judicial review*. Cambridge, MA: Harvard University Press.

Hill v. *Church of Scientology* [1995] 2 S.C.R. 1130.

Hirschl, R. (2007). *Towards juristocracy: The origins and consequences of the new constitutionalism*. Cambridge, MA: Harvard University Press.

Hogg, P. (1985). *Constitutional law of Canada* (2nd ed.). Toronto, ON: Thomson Carswell.

Hogg, P. (1987). The Dolphin Delivery case: The application of the charter to private action. *Saskatchewan Law Review*, *51*(2), 273–280.

Hogg, P. (2012). The brilliant career of Section 7 of the charter. *The Supreme Court Law Review: Osgoode's Annual Constitutional Cases Conference*, *58*(1), 195–210.

Hoskins, Z. (2018). Criminalization and the collateral consequences of conviction. *Criminal Law and Philosophy*, *12*(4), 625–639.

Hutchinson, A. C., & Petter, A. (1988). Private rights/public wrongs: The liberal lie of the charter. *University of Toronto Law Journal*, *38*, 278–297.

Kennedy, D. (1978). The structure of Blackstone's commentaries. *Buffalo Law Review*, *28*(2), 205–382.

Lefort, C. (2006). The permanence of the theologico-political?. In H. De Vries & L. E. Sullivan (Eds.), *Political theologies: Public relations in a post-secular world* (pp. 148–187). New York, NY: Fordham University Press.

McCrudden, C. (2008). Human dignity and judicial interpretation of human rights. *European Journal of International Law*, *19*(4), 655–724.

Michelman, F. (2003). Ida's way: Constructing the respect-worthy governmental system. *Fordham Law Review*, *72*(2), 345–365.

Motha, S. (2018). *Archiving sovereignty*. Ann Arbor, MI: University of Michigan Press.

Pavlich, G. (2007). The lore of criminal accusation. *Criminal Law and Philosophy*, *1*(1), 79–97.

Pavlich, G. (2022). Reframing colonial law's criminally accused persons. *Studies in Law, Politics and Society*, *87*(A), 1–18.

Peller, G., & Tushnet, M. (2003). State action and a new birth of freedom. *Georgetown Law Journal*, *92*, 779.

Reference Re: BC Motor Vehicle Act [1985] 2 S.C.R. 486.

Ricoeur, P. (2000). *The just* (D. Pellauer, Trans.). Chicago, IL: University of Chicago Press.

R. v. *Malmo-Levine*; *R.* v. *Caine* [2003] 3 S.C.R. 571.

R. v. *Morgentaler* [1988] 1 S.C.R. 30.

RWDSU v. *Dolphin Delivery* [1986] 2 S.C.R. 573.
Sandel, M. J. (1984). The procedural republic and the unencumbered self. *Political Theory*, *12*(1), 81–96.
Shelley v. *Kraemer* [1948] 334 U.S. 1.
Singer, J. W. (2012). Subprime: Why a free and democratic society needs law. *Harvard Civil Rights-Civil Liberties Law Review*, *47*, 141–167.
Singer, J. W., & Saidel-Goley, I. (2018). Things invisible to see: State action and private property. *Texas A&M Law Review*, *5*, 439–504.
Sunstein, C. R. (2002). State action is always present. *Chicago Journal of International Law*, *3*, 465–469.
The Constitution Act, 1982, being Schedule B to the Canada Act 1982 (UK), 1982, c 11.
Van der Walt, J. (2012). Law and the space of appearance in Arendt's thought. In C. McCorkindale & M. Goldoni, *Hannah Arendt and the law* (pp. 63–88). Oxford: Hart.
Van der Walt, J. (2014). *The horizontal effect revolution and the question of sovereignty*. Boston, MA: De Gruyter.
Veitch, S. (2007). *Law and irresponsibility: On the legitimation of human suffering*. Oxford: Routledge-Cavendish (Taylor & Francis).
Weinrib, L. (2004). Human dignity as a rights-protecting principle. *National Journal of Constitutional Law*, *17*, 219–239.
Williams, A. T. (2007). Human rights and law: Between sufferance and insufferability. *Law Quarterly Review*, *122*, 132–157.

CHAPTER 6

THE BIOPOLITICS OF SETTLER COLONIALISM AND THE LIMITS OF FOUCAULT'S HISTORICAL METHOD

Amy Swiffen and Shoshana Paget

ABSTRACT

This chapter looks at how the concept of biopolitics can be used to understand the settler colonial legal orders. The focus is on the evolution of the definition of 'Indian status' in the Indian Act, *which is the central piece of legislation in Canada's Indian administration regime. Historically, the legal concept of Indian status was used as a way to constitute a population in relation to colonial sovereignty, and later was adapted as a mechanism to internally dividing the population through complex forms of legal domination. Scholars have turned to Michel Foucault's studies of biopolitics and racism to understand how settler colonial sovereignty relates to a population on a territory. This chapter argues that Foucault's analysis was radically historically embedded in a way that shapes its relevance to understanding settler colonialism. In Foucault's original analysis, racism emerges as tool of the state in the relation between territory and sovereignty, which was characteristic in feudal Europe. In settler colonial legal orders such as Canada, however, sovereignty's relation to the population is constituted in the absence of a prior connection to the land.*

Keywords: Biopolitics; settler colonialism; sovereignty; aboriginal law; Michel Foucault; Canada

Interrupting the Legal Person
Studies in Law, Politics, and Society, Volume 87A, 89–102

Published under exclusive licence by Emerald Publishing Limited
ISSN: 1059-4337/doi:10.1108/S1059-43372022000087A006

Recently, there has been a growth in scholarship in political and legal thought that engages with Michael Foucault's analysis of biopolitics to try to understand the operation of settler colonialism (Brigg, 2007; Dietrich, 2017; Griffiths, 2016; Morgensen, 2011; Rifkin, 2009; Young, 2015). Our analysis of settler colonialism in Canada also draws on Foucault's work, in particular his analysis of sovereignty and biopolitics. However, it does not apply it so much as assess its fit as a tool for analysing settler colonial contexts. In this sense, we are interested in considering not only what insights Foucault's thought might yield about colonial contexts,[1] but also how the radical historicity of Foucault's method risks obscuring some of the specificities of settler colonialism. To do this, we consider the relation of law and biopolitics in more detail than Foucault, who primarily investigated how monarchal sovereignty converges with biopower in taking up the population as a concern of the state. In contrast, we are interested in the way that law operates within biopolitics to constitute a population in the first place. Thus, the arguments are fleshed out through an analysis of the *Indian Act* – the central piece of legislation in Canada's settler colonial administrative regime. In particular, we focus on the legal evolution of the meaning of Indian status, which remains a main organising category within this regime. The meaning of 'Indian status' has evolved ambiguously over 150-years in ways that made possible various processes of dispossession and assimilation. At the same time, the proliferation of different types of Indian status shows the limits of Foucault's biopolitical analysis to explain settler colonialism as a historical phenomenon.

Aspects of the changing definition do not fit well with the analysis of biopolitics in Europe. Foucault's studies of racism, for example, analyse how historically sovereignty starts to relate directly to the life of the population that lives on its territory. However, this analysis assumes a historical relation between territory, population and sovereignty that was characteristic of Europe but not of settler colonial legal orders. Foucault's analysis assumes a shared relation to territory that links sovereignty and the population prior to the emergence of biopolitics. In settler colonial contexts, however, the form of sovereignty that emerged in Europe is applied to populations in the absence of a prior relation to territory.[2] Thus, the operation of sovereignty in settler colonial contexts is necessarily different than in Europe, something that may be missed if Foucault's concepts are used without attending to the limits to their transferability introduced by his historical method. As we demonstrate, applying theories of biopolitics to settler colonial contexts requires a historical consciousness that thinks the relation of population, territory and sovereignty in a different way.

THE BIOPOLITICS OF SETTLER COLONIALISM

Michel Foucault developed the concept of biopolitics using a method embedded in a European historical context. However, there are differences in the operation of sovereignty in settler colonial Canada and in Europe, and in particular a different relationship to territory and population. Given this, it is useful to see how the context of European history is assumed in Foucault's conception of biopolitics.

One way of doing this is to identify the ways in which European history informs his analysis. For instance, Foucault devotes some attention to how racism, and race as a social category, are bound up with the workings of sovereignty to the extent they enable a state to relate to the population as an object of governance. In this sense, Foucault's analysis is focussed on the internal operation of states in so far as racism offers a technique of biopower through which sovereignty can regulate and divide the life of a population upon a territory. This biopolitical understanding of racism is a useful analytical framework for understanding the meaning of race and systemic racism within contemporary Western states. However, as elaborated below, this framework assumes a history of feudalism and Monarchical sovereignty out of which this relation emerges. The biopolitics of settler colonialism, in contrast, involves sovereignty relating to the (Indigenous) population without this same relation to territory.[3] In what follows, we outline Foucault's analysis of biopolitics and racism in more detail to show how it is conditioned by European history, which limits its transferability to studies of settler colonialism.

Foucault mostly elaborates the analysis of biopolitics in *The History of Sexuality* (Foucault, 1990), and lectures *Society Must Be Defended* (Foucault, 2003) and *Security, Territory, Population* (Foucault, 2007), which focus almost exclusively on Europe. In these studies, Foucault traces the rise of the bourgeois class, the emergence of 'race wars', as well as the intersection of disciplinary power and biopower. He refers directly to colonisation only in passing, in particular recognising that strategies of colonial governments can 'boomerang' back to Europe (Foucault, 2003, p. 103). This suggestive but fleeting comment is Foucault's most substantive engagement with colonisation in the context of biopolitics. For the most part, he concentrates on the emergence of biopolitics in Europe, or as he phrases it, the 'basic phenomena of the nineteenth century [when] the biological came under state control' (Foucault, 2003, p. 240). This phenomenon involves an historical process where territorial sovereignty and biopower are 'superimposed' through mechanisms that are simultaneously disciplining of individuals and managing of a population (Foucault, 2003, p. 239). Biopower is associated with the regulation and fostering of collective life. It differs from sovereign power, which operates through the power of death, that is, by either taking life or letting live. In bringing death, sovereign power is excessive and spectacularly destructive of life. In contrast, biopower operates not by killing but by fostering certain forms of life and letting others die (Foucault, 1990, p. 138). In *Society Must Be Defended*, for example, Foucault argues the specificity of modern racism lies in how it is bound up with biopower as a 'technology of power' (p. 258), used to divide the population and differentiate subpopulations. In his discussions, Foucault (2003) shows how race is used by European states as a technique for dividing and sorting individuals (pp. 255–256). Further, he argues racism serves to justify the persistence of the 'death-function' of sovereignty 'in the economy of biopower' (Foucault, 2003, p. 258). In other words, racism justifies the death-bringing aspect of state power, which comes to intersect with biopower through the idea that the death of others 'makes one biologically stronger insofar as one is … an element in a unitary living plurality' (Foucault, 2003, pp. 258–259). Racism is therefore bound up with the workings of a biopolitical state in so far as it is 'obliged' to use race ('the elimination of races and the purification of the race') as a normative justification for the exercise of sovereign power that brings death to individuals or groups (Foucault, 2003, p. 258).

FOUCAULT'S TERRITORIAL ASSUMPTIONS

The limit to the transferability of Foucault's analysis of biopolitics and racism to settler colonial contexts lies in the historicity of his method, which produces concepts that necessarily assume some historical antecedents based on their original setting. Put simply, the focus of Foucault's studies of biopolitics was on a shift from monarchal sovereignty's relation to territory to a relation to the population that dwells upon that territory. He describes, 'From the Middle Ages to the sixteenth century, sovereignty is not exercised on things, but first of all on a territory, and consequently on the subjects who inhabit it' (Foucault, 2007, p. 96). This is the historical backdrop of the analysis, one of European monarchal sovereignty. Similarly, in discussing a text on demography by 'the first great theorist of what we would call biopolitics' Foucault (2007) notes 'we again encounter the problem of the sovereign here, but the sovereign is no longer someone who exercises his power over a territory *on the basis of* a geographical localization of his political sovereignty' (pp. 22–23). The new operation of sovereignty Foucault (2007) is identifying in this passage involves a process where 'territorial sovereignty becomes the architect of the disciplined space [and] the regulator of a milieu' (p. 29). Hence, his focus is on forms of governance that emerge *from* a 'territorial system of power founded and developed on the basis of a territorial domination defined by feudalism' (Foucault, 2007, p. 64). These phrasings reflect how Foucault assumed monarchal sovereignty as historically prior to biopolitics because the history of feudal Europe was the backdrop against which biopolitical sovereignty is thrown into relief. The historical condition out of which 'power's hold over life' emerges is assumed a priori in the ensuing conception (Foucault, 2003, pp. 249–250).

Overall, therefore, Foucault's analysis of biopolitics considers how a relation between sovereignty and population emerges out of a prior relation of territory characteristic of monarchal sovereignty. Biopolitics in this context represents a change in the relation between sovereignty, territory and the population that was characteristic of European feudal relations. Foucault uncovers how populations are constituted as subjects who dwell upon the territories of former monarchal sovereigns. In settler colonial contexts, however, the prior relation to territory out of which monarchal sovereignty's relation to the population emerges is not present. Thus, Foucault's analysis assumes a historical relation between sovereignty and territory that existed in Europe but not in settler colonial contexts. Sovereignty in settler colonialism lacks the same historical relation to territory as in Europe because it relates to Indigenous peoples and nations that had relations to land before the settler colonial state (Alfred, 1995; Borrows, 2010; Simpson, 2014). At stake in settler colonialism, thus, is not a shift in sovereignty's relation from territory to the population, but the constitution of a relation to a population in the absence of the relation to land that the history of Europe provided. This means the relation between population, sovereignty and territory must be constituted in a different manner than Foucault described. Instead of shifting from a territorial relation to a direct relation to the population, as in Europe, some other operation is required to constitute the population in settler colonialism.

Scholarly attention has noted the affinities between the negative and death-bringing techniques of sovereignty and racism used by liberal states and the assimilationist policies of settler colonial governments (Monaghan, 2013; Morgensen, 2011; Rifkin, 2009; Wolfe, 2006; Young, 2015). Some have also criticised Foucault's discussion of race for not focussing more centrally on racism and instead treating it as a secondary concern. For example, Ann Stoler (2016) points out that in *History of Sexuality* Foucault's main focus is not on analysing racism as a phenomenon in its own right but on its role as 'a *tactic* in the internal fission of society into binary oppositions' (p. 22). She argues racism is interesting to Foucault's analysis of biopolitics only in so far as it is 'a technique of creating "biologized" internal enemies, against whom society must defend itself' (Stoler, 1995, p. 59; 2016, p. 22). Rivera Santana (2018) finds the same in his work on the biopolitics of Queensland, Australia, noting 'Foucault is not interested in racism itself, but rather in its operation and how it presents the foundations of a new 'art of government' – what he calls biopolitics' (p. 227).[4] Weheliye (2014) similarly finds that Foucault only focusses on Nazism to explore the operation of biopower and biopolitics, a solely European phenomenon. He notes Foucault does not explore 'other forms of biopolitics… perfected in colonialism, Indigenous genocide, racialized indentured servitude, and racial slavery, for instance' (p. 59). These scholars respond to substantive gaps in Foucault's studies and have supplemented his account with analyses that are contextualised in global geographies and take into account sex and gender (Morgensen, 2011; Rifkin, 2009).

Our point is a bit different in that we suggest Foucault's radically historical method also presents an inherent limitation to the transferability of his analyses to settler colonial contexts. An application of Foucault's analysis of biopolitics to settler colonial legal orders must to be attentive to the limit of his account in this sense. To illustrate, we look at Canada's *Indian Act* and the legal genealogy of the concept of Indian status that it defines. Scholars have noted the affinity between Canada's policies of assimilation and some of the techniques of racism discussed by Michel Foucault. While we discuss these below, we also want to highlight aspects of Canada's Indian administration regime that do not fit well even into this frame. For example, while the goal of the *Indian Act* was assimilation and eventual disappearance of the 'Indian' population, this has not been its effect. Due largely to various form of Indigenous refusal, Indian status has sub-divided and expanded in ambivalent ways over time such that the Indian population as defined by the *Indian Act* is now growing. The death-bringing and eliminatory aspects of settler colonial law and sovereignty does not account for how Indigenous legalities continue to exist and have variously refused and shaped the settler legal order over time. These historical specificities do not fit neatly with the idea of biopolitics and the techniques of racism as purification that Foucault described. Drawing on Foucault's concepts to understand settler colonialism must be done with an awareness that the European historical context is an assumed ground. Not only is this missing one of the distinguishing features of settler colonialism, it would repeat the colonial gesture of assuming Crown sovereignty's relation to territory.

CONSTITUTING AN 'INDIAN' POPULATION

For multiple centuries, the Canadian state has built a complex Indian administrative regime imposed on Indigenous peoples without voluntary consent freely given (Asch, 2021). The central piece of legislation in this regime is the Indian Act (1985), first passed in 1876. It is based on a settler colonial interpretation of a power transferred from the British Crown to the federal government to govern 'in relation to Indians and lands reserved for Indians' (The Constitution Act, *1982*, s. 91(24)).[5] This was interpreted by politicians, courts and officials to mean the settler state ('Crown sovereignty') had jurisdiction *over* 'Indians', who in turn occupied a ward-like status. The *Indian Act* was passed under this auspice. It consolidated various pieces of legislation that already existed pertaining to Indigenous peoples, which the imperial crown recognised as 'Indians'. The first version of the *Indian Act* attempted to recognise a unitary population of 'Indians' that it could relate to as a population on settler terms. In doing so, it constituted a population in relation to Crown sovereignty in Canada. Note, this is an important difference from European biopolitics in that the category of Indian was not constituted out of a population of subjects who dwelled upon the territory of a pre-existing sovereign. Indigenous nations had their own polities (Simpson, 2014, p. 2). Rather, the form of relation between Crown sovereignty and the Indian population is based on separating Indigenous nations from their territorial sovereignty.

The *Indian Act* was in fact not the first piece of legislation to invoke Indian status. It was defined for the first time in Canada in the earlier *Act for the Better Protection of Lands and Property of the Indians,* which passed in Upper Canada in 1850. The purpose of the legal category in the latter Act was determining eligibility for residency on reserve lands. An 'Indian' was any person 'of Indian blood' who belonged to a 'body or tribe of Indians' (S.P.C., 1850, c. 42, s. V).[6] This formulation reflected the European understandings of race prevalent at the time, which centred around the idea of race as a biological difference that distinguished different types of humans. This biopolitical framework was externally imposed and underpinned the subordination of Indigenous peoples in their relationship to the Canadian state as a population (Simpson, 2007, p. 75). As the nineteenth century progressed, colonial authorities developed increasingly aggressive policies of assimilation that used Indian status as a tool for implementation (Giokas & Groves, 2002, p. 53). These policies restricted Indigenous peoples' forms of association and mobility, and linked the notion of 'Indian community' to specific bases of land, notably, Indian reserves (Starblanket, 2018, p. 6).[7] Sexist provisions were used to divide and regulate the 'Indian population' through targeting female people in discriminatory ways. One of the central mechanisms of this was known as enfranchisement introduced in the *Gradual Civilization Act* in 1857. The Act offered males with Indian status 50 acres of land and a share of their band's annuities in exchange for renouncing Indian status and becoming Canadian citizens (Giokas & Groves, 2002, pp. 53–54).[8] If an Indigenous man was enfranchised in this way his wife and children were also eligible for enfranchisement. The 1869 *Gradual Enfranchisement Act* [S.C. 1869] took this further and made it so women with Indian status who married non-Indian men were automatically 'enfranchised', which meant losing their status and band membership, along with any children of the marriage (S.C., 1869, c. 6). These components of the Indian administration regime were incorporated in 1876 in the *Indian Act*, which further accelerated assimilation policies targeting the 'Indian' population (Giokas & Groves, 2002, p. 54). In particular, the definition of Indian status was tightened and defined explicitly as 'any *male* person of Indian blood' as well as his wife and children (S.C., 1919–20, c. 26, s. 2). New marrying out provisions were also added specifying that women would be automatically lose Indian status as of the date of a marriage to a non-Indian man. If the husband of a women with Indian status died or abandoned her, she would also lose her status. These policies served to disconnect many Indigenous women and children from their communities (Simpson, 2007, p. 74).

Several significant changes were made to the *Indian Act* in 1951 that further developed these processes. The definition of Indian was changed again. This time the reference to blood was eliminated and replaced by the concept of 'registration' (*Indian Act S.C.*, 1951, c. 29). Registration meant being eligible for inclusion in the new federally created and controlled Indian Register. Up until that point, individual band councils kept their own membership lists. The Register was the first attempt by the settler colonial state to create a centralised list of the Indian population. By this time, since so many women and their children had lost Indian status over generations due to enfranchisement and marrying out provisions, many people were left off the official Register. The 1951 amendments further compounded the sexism of the *Indian Act* in other ways, for example, by introducing the so-called double mother rule that stipulated a person would lose Indian status at age 21 if their mother and grandmother had obtained status through marriage (Giokas & Groves, 2002, p. 57). The biopolitical goals of these provisions are clear. They were techniques designed to eliminate the 'Indian population', first constituted through a racist logic linked to blood, and later as a legal entitlement to registration created by the *Indian Act* itself.

Following the 1951 amendments, Indigenous women launched multiple court cases to challenge the sections of the *Indian Act* that discriminated based on sex. As Audra Simpson (2007) describes, these women had also faced discrimination from within their communities, finally resorting to the settler courts after they

> had unsuccessfully petitioned their band council governments to let them return, to raise their children and exercise their rights as Indians. The band council governments upheld the Indian Act and challenged the women to bring their case to the courts. (p. 72)

In 1971, Jeannette Lavell brought an action claiming the *Indian Act* violated the equality clause in the 1960 *Canadian Bill of Rights* by discriminating on the basis of sex. The case was linked to that of Yvonne Bedard, who lost her status and right to inherit reserve land when she married a non-Indian man in 1964 (*Bedard* v. *Isaac et al.* 1971, 601, ON SC). The cases were heard by the Supreme Court of Canada, which ruled against the women and upheld the 'marrying out' provision (12(1)(b)) of the *Indian Act*. The Court sated the women were not being discriminated against because they had gained equal rights as Canadian citizens when they were striped on their Indian status. In any case, it also stated the federal government had the constitutional power to manage Indian affairs and this could not be superseded by a statute, even one that enshrined civil rights (*Attorney General of Canada* v. *Lavell* [1974] S.C.R. 1349). In the wake of this decision, Sandra Lovelace launched a challenge to the *Indian Act* through the United Nations Human Rights Committee. Her reserve community had continued to apply the *Indian Act* legislation to deny female members of the community who married out the right to acquire property on the reserve. After seeing in Bedard that the Canadian courts would be no help, Lovelace went to the UN and argued this situation violated the International Covenant on Civil and Political Rights.[9] In 1981, the UN Human Rights Committee agreed, finding Canada in violation of the Covenant (Bayefsky, 1982).[10]

This international shame motivated the Canadian government to start to address sex discrimination in the *Indian Act*. First, through Bill C-31 in 1987, which ended the marrying out and double mother rules. The concept of enfranchisement was also abolished. The result was thousands of women and their children who had lost Indian status were reinstated. However, Bill C-31 also gave band councils the authority to create their own membership codes. The band councils in some communities chose to challenge the right of women to be reinstated by excluding them from community membership; some community leaders argued it was now their tradition to exclude women who married out (see Green, 2004).[11] Audra Simpson's work addresses this conflict around the politics of membership in the context of Kahnawà:ke territory, located on the south shore of the St. Lawrence River, near Montreal, Quebec. Simpson's analysis considers the impact of colonial interventions on local Indigenous politics, such as the expropriation of riverfront land that was central to Kahnawa'kehró:non identity (and the failure of the courts to prevent it). Her work also examines how the *Indian Act* made it possible for non-Indigenous men to own reserve land by gaining Indian status through marriage. She argues this larger context is an important piece to understanding the refusal of some Indigenous communities to recognise women who had previously lost their status. Simpson's conclusion is that the refusal was both discriminatory and resistance to colonisation. Previous interventions from settler state had impacted the meaning of membership within the community, and some tenants of the *Indian Act* had been assimilated into the social fabric (Simpson, 2014, p. 57).

At the same time, Bill C-31 still continued to treat males and females differently. For individuals with one parent with Indian status, their ability to pass on their own status was different depending on if the parent was male or female. Thus, shortly after Bill C-31, Indigenous women asserted that they continued to be affected by sex-based discrimination. In 1989, Sharon McIvor launched a challenge to the new provisions. She had lost her Indian status when she married a non-Indian man but was reinstated following Bill C-31, yet her children were still more limited in their ability to pass on their status than their cousins, who were the children of McIvor's brother (*McIvor* v. *Canada (Registrar of Indian & Northern Affairs)*, 2009).[12] In 2009, the British Columbia Court of Appeal (BCCA) agreed and ordered Canada to expand the entitlement to Indian status in order to fully get rid of the discrimination against women.[13] The government's response was *The Gender Equity in Indian Registration Act* or Bill C-3 in 2011, which undid more of the sexism in the status provisions (Giokas & Groves, 2002, p. 57). For instance, Bill C-3 established new categories of Indian status, this time to recognise individuals whose grandmothers had been enfranchised. Over 174,500 individuals became newly registered under Bill C-3.

Despite these changes, some sex discrimination was still carried forward in that the new provisions only applied to individuals born after 1951.[14] This cut-off meant women were still more limited in their ability to pass on Indian status compared to male counterparts. Therefore, in 2015 Canada lost another court challenge by Indigenous women. In the *Descheneaux* case, the Superior Court of Quebec directed the federal government to finally correct the registration provisions to end all sex inequities.[15] The result was Bill S-3, which came into effect in 2019 (Bill S-3, 2017). This amendment ensures grandchildren and great-grandchildren of women who lost status as a result of marrying out are entitled to registration. It also ensures female children born out of wedlock are entitled to registration, as well as their descendants.[16] Thus, all descendants of women who were removed from band lists or were not considered Indians because of marrying out going back to the 1869 *Gradual Enfranchisement Act* are now entitled to Indian status, as are their descendants. The Canadian Government has estimated between 750,000 and 1.3 million people in Canada could be entitled to registration under Bill S-3 (Crown-Indigenous Relations and Northern Affairs Canada, 2018).[17]

BIOPOLITICS OF INDIAN STATUS

Among the historical and legal developments above are several aspects of settler colonial biopolitics that risk being overlooked if Foucault's assumptions about European territorial sovereignty are carried forward into settler colonial contexts. First, there is no shared historical background of monarchal sovereignty and population sharing a link to territory as in feudal Europe. Indigenous peoples were not dwelling upon the territory of monarchal sovereigns who took them up as a population. They were instead dwelling upon the territories of their own polities and political organisations. Indigenous peoples could not be *a* population in relation to Crown sovereignty in a biopolitical sense until Indian status came into being to sustain the relation through legal domination. Indigenous peoples could perhaps be said to be populations in relation to their own existing forms of legal authority. However, to establish this relation with the settler colonial sovereignty without a prior relation to territory, the legal concept of 'Indian' was used as a tool to constitute a population out of diverse societies and without voluntary consent. Second, this legal process 'set Indigenous peoples up for governmental regulation' (Simpson, 2014, p. 21; see also Morgensen, 2011) using techniques of biopower in Foucault's sense, yet the outcome has not been elimination or purification. Instead, the Indian population has expanded and the concept of Indian status has internally differentiated. In part, this is due to repeated forms of refusal by Indigenous women using instruments of the settler legal system against itself (Simpson, 2014, p. 155).[18]

Therefore, while Foucault describes biopolitics in terms of sovereignty relating to the population as an object of governance upon its territory, in settler colonialism the movement does not unfold in the same direction. As demonstrated by the discussion of Indian status, Crown sovereignty does not come to relate to the 'Indian population' from a prior historical relation to territory. Rather, the relation to the population is constituted first to ease the appropriation of territory through a legal form of diminished personhood, that is, the creation of Indian status. In this context, Foucault's analysis of racism is very relevant because the policies of assimilation that were built upon the legal domination of the Indian population reflect techniques of internal purification that he described. Yet, the initial biopolitical operation of settler colonial sovereignty involved constituting an Indian population through a legal form of capture, not through a shift from territoriality to the governance of the population. Put differently, instead of a shift from a territorial base to a relation to the population upon it, a supplemental or additional operation was required to constitute an Indian population in the first place.

CONCLUSION

There is a tendency in applications of Foucault's work to see biopolitics as synonymous with sovereignty, that is, both are equated with a negative force outside of life that is applied to life.[19] From such a perspective, biopolitics is only visible when it manifests as external to life and is imposed from the outside. While this framing captures a fundamental aspect of settler colonial biopolitics it does not capture the complete picture. As the discussion of the *Indian Act* shows, biopolitics did not purify the population, but rather created an expanding and internally diverse form of diminished legal personhood. Indigenous peoples are not related to Crown sovereignty in the way of the peasant populations of Europe because of the absence of the prior shared relation of territory. It could only be after the *Indian Act* was imposed and Indian status came into being that a biopolitical relation between the settler colonial sovereignty and Indigenous peoples as a single population was possible. This does not emerge from a shared relation to territory as the sovereignty Foucault was studying. It is not conditioned by a historical link to land, but rather the absence of one. Thus, whereas Foucault describes how territorial sovereignty shifts to governing the life as a population, in settler colonialism things do not happen in this direction. First, the legal concept of 'Indian' had to be developed based on European understandings of race; it was then applied to diverse Indigenous peoples to constitute a population that became centrally defined in 1951. This is why as Douglas Sanders (1972) pointed out the *Indian Act* continued to use a racial term – Indian – to signify a group that is no longer determined by blood criteria. This politics of recognition had first divided Indigenous life and then tied it to reserve land. This can be missed if concepts drawn from Foucault's analysis are applied without attending to how they assume a particular historical context.

Foucault's analyses of biopolitics are definitely illuminating for understanding these dynamics of biopolitics in settler colonial contexts, though this was never his focus. Yet, his historical method does present an inherent limit to its transferability to other settings. It is necessarily embedded in European history where monarchal sovereignty is the historical background out of which the application of biopower by the state to populations emerges. This conception of biopolitics as emanating from a prior relation to territorial sovereignty does not apply in settler colonial contexts in the same way. The assumption of a shared history of territorial sovereignty (stemming from feudal history in Europe) is not present and remains contested. The analysis of Canada's *Indian Act* shows how settler colonial sovereignty operates differently due to its unique (lacking) relation to territory. The specificity of settler colonial biopolitics is based on responding to the lack of historical ground for sovereignty's particular claim. Foucault's analysis of racism is important because the policies of assimilation enacted through the *Indian Act* aimed at eliminating Indigenous peoples through biopolitical techniques of internal purification. Yet, on its own this framing does not account for the supplemental operation of settler colonial sovereignty, which involves the creation of a form of diminished legal personhood in the absence of a history of territorial relation. A reading of settler colonial sovereignty only as a mechanism of biopolitical purification misses how a population needed to be constituted in the first place, as well as the processes of expansion and diversification of Indian status, which has not died out but acquired a life of its own.

NOTES

1. This approach is inspired by Robert Nichols' (2014) work on the colonialism of political theory.
2. The implication is not that sovereignty is unitary, localised or came from Europe. At issue is the specific form of sovereignty reflected in European colonisation, which became the basis for settler states. Indigenous forms of nationhood existed and continue to operate. See Alfred, (2006) and Simpson (2014).
3. I am referring to Indigenous legal cultures and forms of law that existed and continue to exist.
4. 'The discursive practice of racism is used as a "strategy of war" to eliminate the undesired races' (Foucault).
5. The Indian Act is a form of administrative law. Thus, band council governments are understood by the courts as delegated authority emanating from federal jurisdiction.
6. This definition included those descended from, married to or adopted by those of 'Indian blood' (S.P.C., 1850, c. 74, s. X).
7. This arrangement was originally envisioned by the settler state as a temporary structure that would disappear as Canada's assimilation policies progressed (Nichols, 2018, pp. 8–9).

8. To be eligible for voluntary enfranchisement an individual had to be able to read and write, be free of debt and be of 'good character'.

9. Lovelace charged that the Indian Act did not comply with section 27 of the International Covenant on Civil and Political Rights.

10. Another significant event occurred in 1982 when the Canadian constitution was amended to include the *Canadian Charter of Rights and Freedoms*, which contained provisions guaranteeing the equality of males and females. Section 15 of the Charter states 'every individual is equal before and under the law and has the right to the equal protection and benefit of the law without discrimination based on race, national or ethnic origin, colour, religion, sex, age, or mental or physical disability' (*The Constitution Act*, 1982, c 11, s. 15).

11. For other accounts of this history see Coulthard, 2014, pp. 79–104 and Simpson, 2014, p. 56; see also Barker, 2008; Lawrence, 2003; Palmater, 2011).

12. McIvor was reinstated under section 6(1)(c).

13. In 2006, McIvor won her case. The Crown appealed and soon after the government ended the federally funded Court Challenges programme, which funded court cases that supported language and equality rights under Canada's constitution. McIvor's case had been supported by the programme but she raised funds and defended her own case.

14. The ways the various types of Indian status carry forward sex discrimination are complex. For a technical description see this fact sheet on the 1951 cut-off: https://www.rcaanc-cirnac.gc.ca/eng/1540403451139/1568898699984.

15. The Superior Court of Quebec ruled provisions relating to Indian registration under the *Indian Act* were unconstitutional because they perpetuated a difference in treatment between Indian women as compared to Indian men, as well as their respective descendants. See Crown-Indigenous Relations and Northern Affairs Canada (2018). Collaborative Process on Indian Registration, Band Membership and First Nation Citizenship: Consultation Plan: Background on Indian Registration. Retrieved from the Government of Canada website: https://www.rcaanc-cirnac.gc.ca/eng/1540405608208/1568898474141#_Bill_C-31_and.

16. Some changes from Bill S-3 in response to the situations identified by the Superior Court of Quebec in the *Descheneaux* case took effect on 22 December, 2017. The rest came into effect on 15 August 2019 after a process of consultation.

17. The estimate is based on the number of individuals who self-reported as having North American Indian ancestry or identity in the 2016 Census.

18. As Simpson describes, it is also due to various Indigenous communities refusing the elimination from territory by resisting legal acts of the Canadian government

19. For example, a recent discussion of post-colonial literary culture argues biopolitics is applied by sovereign power to Indigenous peoples in order to 'regularize a population according to the perceived existence of norms' (Griffiths, 2016, p. 1). A study on the surveillance practices in the early years of colonisation in Canada, argues 'biopolitical ordering produces initial categories for the governance and elimination of Indigenous populations' (Monaghan, 2013, p. 492).

REFERENCES

Alfred, T. (1995). *Heeding the voices of our ancestors: Kahnawake Mohawk politics and the rise of native nationalism*. Oxford: Oxford University Press.

Alfred, T. (2006). Sovereignty—An inappropriate concept. In *The indigenous experience: Global perspectives* (pp. 322–336). Toronto, ON: Canadian Scholars' Press.

Asch, M. (2021). Self-determination and treaty-making: consent and the resolution of political relations between first nations and Canada. In *Futures of federalism*. UTP (forthcoming).

Attorney General of Canada v. *Lavell*, 1974, S.C.R. 1349.

Barker, J. (2008). Gender, sovereignty, rights: Native women's activism against social inequality and violence in Canada. *American Quarterly*, *60*(2), 259–266.

Bayefsky, A. (1982). The Human Rights Committee and the case of Sandra Lovelace. *Canadian Yearbook of International Law*, *20*, 244–266.

Bedard v. *Isaac et al.*, 1971 CanLII 601 (ON SC).

Bill S-3, 2017. Canada. *Bill S-3, An Act to amend the Indian Act in response to the Superior Court of Quebec decision in Descheneaux c. Canada (Procureur general) R.S.*, 2017 c. 25.

Borrows, J. (2010). Canada's indigenous constitution. Toronto, ON: University of Toronto Press.

Brigg, M. (2007). Biopolitics meets terrapolitics: Political ontologies and governance in settler-colonial Australia. *Australian Journal of Political Science*, *42*(3), 403–417.

Canada. *An Act for the Better Protection of Lands and Property of the Indians in Lower Canada*, S.P.C. 1850.

Canada. *An Act for the Gradual Enfranchisement of Indians, the Better Management of Indian Affairs, and to Extend the Provisions of the Act 31st Victoria*, S.C. 1869, c. 6.

Canada. *Indian Act 1985* R.S.C., 1985, c. I-5.

Canada. *Indian Act S.C.* 1951, c. 29.

Canada. *Indian Act S.C.* 1919–1920, c. 26, s. 2.

Canada. *The Constitution Act*, 1982, s. 91(24).

Canada. *The Constitution Act*, 1982, Schedule B, 1982, c 11.

Crown-Indigenous Relations and Northern Affairs Canada. (2018). Collaborative process on Indian registration, band membership and first nation citizenship: Consultation plan: Background on Indian registration. Retrieved from https://www.rcaanc-cirnac.gc.ca/eng/1540405608208/1568898474141#_Bill_C-31

Dietrich, R. (2017). The biopolitical logics of settler colonialism and disruptive relationality. *Cultural Studies ↔ Critical Methodologies*, *17*(1), 67–77.

Descheneaux c. Canada (Procureur Général), 2015 QCCS 3555.

Foucault, M. (1990). *The history of sexuality*. New York, NY: Vintage Books.

Foucault, M. (2003). *"Society must be defended": Lectures at the College de France 1975–6* (M. Bertanti & A. Fontana, Eds., D. Macey, Trans.). New York, NY: Picador.

Foucault, M. (2007). *Security, territory, population: Lectures at the College de France 1977–78*. New York, NY: Picador.

Giokas, J., & Groves, R. K. (2002). Collective and individual recognition in Canada. In P. L. A. H. Chartrand (Ed.), *Who are Canada's aboriginal peoples?* (pp. 41–82). Saskatoon: Purich Publishing Ltd.

Green, J. (2004). Balancing strategies: Aboriginal women and constitutional rights in Canada. In A. Dobrowolsky & V. Hart (Eds.), *Women making constitutions: New perspectives and comparative perspectives* (pp. 36–51) New York, NY: Palgrave.

Griffiths, M. R. (2016). Biopolitical correspondences: Settler nationalism, thanatopolitics, and the perils of hybridity. *Australian Literary Studies*, *26*, 20–42.

Lawrence, B. (2003). Gender, race and the regulation of identity in the U.S. and Canada. *Hypatia*, *18*(2), 3–31

McIvor v. *Canada* (Registrar of Indian and Northern Affairs), 2009 BCCA.

Monaghan, J. (2013). Settler governmentality and racializing surveillance in Canada's north-west. *Canadian Journal of Sociology*, *38*(4), 487–508.

Morgensen, S. L. (2011). The biopolitics of settler colonialism: Right here, right now. *Settler Colonial Studies*, *1*(1), 52–76.

Nichols, J. (2018). *Sui generis sovereignties: The relationship between treaty interpretation and Canadian sovereignty*. Canada in international law at 150 and beyond – Paper No. 1, Centre for International Governance Innovation.

Nichols, R. (2014). Contract and usurpation: Enfranchisement and racial governance in settler-colonial contexts. In S. Audra (Ed.), *Theorizing native studies* (pp. 99–121). Durham: Duke University Press.

Rivera Santana, C. (2018). Colonization, coloniality and bio-power: Biopolitics in Queensland, Australia. *Cultural Studies*, *32*(2), 223–239.

Rifkin, M. (2009). Indigenizing Agamben: Rethinking sovereignty in light of the "peculiar" status of native peoples. *Cultural Critique*, *73*, 88–124.

Sanders, D. E. (1972). The Bill of Rights and Indian status. *University of British Columbia Law Review*, *7*(1), 81–105.

Simpson, A. (2007). On ethnographic refusal: Indigeneity, 'voice' and colonial citizenship. *Junctures: The Journal for Thematic Dialogue*, *9*, 67–80.

Simpson, A. (2014). *Mohawk interruptus: Political life across the borders of settler states*. Durham: Duke University Press.

Starblanket, G. (2018). Complex accountabilities: Deconstructing "the community" and engaging indigenous feminist research methods. *American Indian Culture and Research Journal*, *42*(4), 1–20.

Stoler, A. L. (1995). *Race and the education of desire*. Durham, NC: Duke University Press.

Stoler, A. L. (2016). *Duress: Imperial durabilities in our times*. Durham, NC: Duke University Press.

Young, B. (2015). Killing the Indian in the child: Death, cruelty, and subject-formation in the Canadian Indian residential school system. *Mosaic: An Interdisciplinary Critical Journal*, *48*(4), 63–76.

Weheliye, A. G. (2014). *Habeas viscus: Racializing assemblages, biopolitics, and black feminist theories of the human*. Durham, NC: Duke University Press.

Wolfe, P. (2006). Settler colonialism and the elimination of the native. *Journal of Genocide Research*, *8*(4), 387–409.

CHAPTER 7

INTERRUPTED BY DEATH: THE LEGAL PERSONHOOD AND NON-PERSONHOOD OF CORPSES

James R. Martel

ABSTRACT

In In Re Widening of Beekman Street, *a nineteenth century legal case in New York State which involved questions of who owned the bodies of the dead – whether it was the state, the church who owned the land where they were buried or the relatives of the deceased – we see an interesting legal aporia. Claims of ownership were complicated by the idea that the dead perhaps owned themselves, having once been full legal subjects. In this and other legal cases in US law (with similar results in the UK as well) a kind of compromise is reached where, as the body decays, the question of its self-ownership becomes increasingly settled in favour of other parties. Yet, even in such cases, the body and its sense of personhood lingers to haunt, as it were, the certainties of law about who precisely owns whom The uncertainties that are made manifest among the dead have their equivalents among the living as well; the presence of slavery at the time meant that in some cases even living persons did not own themselves. In this mix of overlapping forms of self and other ownership then, we see an anxiety in the law, one that it must settle definitively even as the very terms of legal personhood resist the very closure that the law seeks.*

Keywords: *In re Widening of Beekman Street*; corpses; self-ownership; legal personhood; burial; property

Interrupting the Legal Person
Studies in Law, Politics, and Society, Volume 87A, 103–118

Published under exclusive licence by Emerald Publishing Limited
ISSN: 1059-4337/doi:10.1108/S1059-43372022000087A007

INTRODUCTION

When it comes to its relationship to the living, the law confidently expounds on the nature of its subjects, on the rights and limits of their personhood and how those terms can be regulated and adjudicated. But when it comes to the dead everything seems to change. The law wants to have jurisdiction in all matters and in all forms of life and death alike but death tends to upend and complicate both the law's jurisdiction and its competency. It seems that when it comes to dead bodies, the law does not quite know what to say. In this chapter, I will explore the question of legal subjectivity through a discussion of the law's interaction with death. Death, I will argue, interrupts the legal subject like nothing else. By examining a series of court cases and court briefs and expert opinions from US law I will show how the moment of death instigates a transition away from personhood. The law deems personhood as such to be decreasingly present as the body decomposes. Yet, there is a way that the body (or its remains) retains some link to legal personhood whereby one could say that the legal person is 'haunted' by the dead body it has become.[1] The corpse never quite becomes an object like other objects even as it ceases (and increasingly so over time) to be a subject either. This state of being, which one court called 'quasi property' (but could just as easily therefore be called 'quasi personhood' as well) is a marked interruption not only of legal personhood but I would argue further of law itself (*Pierce* v. *Proprietors of Swan Point Cemetery*, p. 1125). Confronted with a self that isn't quite a self and an object that isn't quite an object, the law must explain how this strange thing can remain within its scope. And this is precisely where the radical implications of this situation come into play; by insisting that this thing *is* a legal subject/object, the law holds onto something that deeply subverts it, bringing a radical aporia into its heart. In doing so, the very categories that the law would (but can't quite) use to subject the dead body are themselves called into questions instead. Given that, at the time of this writing, we are in the middle of the worst pandemic in 100 years, the question of death and law's relationship to it, of who, if anyone 'owns' the dead body and what agency that body has as itself, seems especially critical to understand.

Two thinkers help to set the stage for this conversation: Walter Benjamin and Michel Foucault. Benjamin gives us a good understanding of the way that the corpse as such threatens (however strange this may seem) the law and the state. Foucault helps to historicise this argument by showing how the rise of what he calls biopolitics creates a regime in which death has a particular and troubled relationship to political and legal power. Reading these two thinkers in tandem helps to set the stage for the legal readings that I will then engage with.

BENJAMIN: THE DEFIANCE OF THE CORPSE

To make this argument, let me begin with Benjamin. In his 'Critique of Violence', the essay where he spends the most time talking about the law, Benjamin argues that law is a subset of what he calls 'mythic violence'. Mythic violence refers to the way that the law, among other institutions of power, has no ontological or absolute basis (we see this very clearly in the case law that I will turn to shortly when recourse to mystical ancient and 'uncorrupted' common law is seen as a basis for the law's authority).

This kind of mythic self-assertion is 'violent' (the original German word *gewalt* speaks more about force than physical violence) because the law must produce its own right and authority out of thin air. For Benjamin, the law does not operate for the benefit its subjects (as it asserts) but rather only for itself. Indeed, the violence of this self-assertion necessitates a more literal violence that is promulgated onto the bodies of (some of) its subjects in order to produce and demonstrate its power and authority. Thus, Benjamin (1996) tells us that:

> If violence, violence crowned by fate, is the origin of law, then it may be readily supposed that where the highest violence, that over life and death, occurs in the legal system, the origins of law jut manifestly and fearsomely into existence. [The purpose of capital punishment] is not to punish the infringement of law but to establish new law. (p. 242)

Here, we see that the law establishes itself via capital punishment. Even in countries that formally have ended the practice of capital punishment, the police still kill people, and in particular – at least in European and settler colonial societies that came from Europe – people of colour. For Benjamin, this kind of violence is not accidental but rather necessary to maintain legal and political power.

For Benjamin, mythic violence is ubiquitous but we are not fated to it. In the 'Critique' he opposes mythic violence with divine violence, a counterforce that comes from God and which serves to unmake the mythic violence that is done in its name. Divine violence is not something that human beings can engage in but it does open up a space in the world by which human beings can resist their own mythic tendencies. Thanks to this counterforce, every object in the world, including the objects that are our bodies, resist the projections that are put onto them (commodity fetishism being a central aspect of mythic violence). For every instance of projection there is a force of counter-projection, a form of assertion that produces, not so much the truth (since for Benjamin this can never really be known), but at least a counter to the false truths that subjects and objects of law are forced to otherwise bear.

Although for Benjamin all bodies resist, that resistance is undermined by the great seductive power of what he calls the 'phantasmagoria', the miasma of promises, lies, phantasms and other alluring aspects of myth that beguile us and lower our resistance to mythic authority. Living persons are constantly being assaulted by an entire network of pseudo authorities that convinces us that the lies of mythic forms of power – legal forms very much included – are in fact true, good and decent (or rational or natural, etc.). Even the most ardent resister of law and capitalism can't help succumbing to some extent to the phantasmagoria. The idolatrous forms that we worship are our legacy as descendants (in Benjamin's highly Eurocentric, theological and Abrahamic viewpoint) of the Fall of Adam. Since the Fall, human beings have no access to truth. In our desperate desire to restore an Edenic connection to what we've lost, we are highly susceptible for what passes for truth in this postlapsarian context.

Benjamin tells us that with the dead, everything is different. For one thing, the dead do not participate in the mythic economy of the phantasmagoria. Phantasmic projections are wasted on the corpse. Given its inert and rotting form, the dead body fails to reflect back mythic projection, offering nothing but resistance to those phantasms (for an elaboration on this claim, see Martel, 2018). Benjamin argues that the corpse becomes increasingly object like as it decomposes. This claim, as I will show further in this chapter, is almost the perfect mirror for what the law – US based law, anyway – says about dead bodies as well. But whereas for the law this transformation is seen as a loss of personhood, for Benjamin it is in a sense the ultimate culmination of our personhood. In his *Origin of German Tragic Drama* Benjamin (1998) tells us:

> And if it is in death that the spirit becomes free, in the manner of spirits, it is not until then that the body too comes properly into its own. For this much is self-evident: the allegorization of the physis can only be carried through in all its vigour in respect of the corpse. And the characters of the *Trauerspiel* [the German baroque plays that are the study of Benjamin's book] die, because it is only thus, as corpses, that they can enter into the homeland of allegory. It is not for the sake of immortality that they meet their end, but for the sake of the corpse. (pp. 217–218)

Rather than trying to read out the dead body from life, as so much of normative theory and practice will do (burial and cremation can both be read as seeking to accomplish just that), Benjamin sees how the dead body is 'most itself' *qua* dead precisely because it is least overwritten by phantasms of identity and subjectivity.[2] He tells us that as a corpse, the body enters into 'the homeland of allegory'. Insofar as allegory is for Benjamin a trope that maximally challenges grand narratives of normative subjectivity, the corpse can be read as an allegorical figure for the human being more generally. In this mode, one that seems to increase as the body decomposes, the dead body is especially and perhaps even ultimately interruptive for modes of legal personhood.

For Benjamin, unlike as with law, there is no conflict between the body as subject and the body as object. Even as the dead body becomes more object like as it decomposes, for Benjamin it does not lose its subjective status. In this way, Benjamin refuses any sense of the absolutely incommensurability between the living and the dead. Thus, once again in *Origin of German Tragic Drama* Benjamin (1998) writes:

> Seen from the point of view of death, the product of the corpse is life. It is not only in the loss of limbs, not only in the changes of the aging body, but in all the processes of elimination and purification that everything corpse-like falls away from the body piece by piece. It is no accident that precisely nails and hair, which are cut away as dead matter from the living body, continue to grow on the corpse. There is in the physis, in the memory itself, a *memento mori*. (p. 218)

In this way, the corpse is not entirely removed from life. It continues to generate and to change, even if that change is one that we tend to view as repellent. Here, the body remains agentic. Indeed, I would argue that it can be claimed that the dead body is far *more* agentic than the living body for Benjamin precisely because it becomes immune from and entirely resistant to the kinds of de-agentifying forces that constantly assault the living subjects of the phantasmagoria. Rather than creating a conflict for the living subject, the dead body resolves that conflict for Benjamin by having its subjectivity and objectivity effectively merge into one.

In this way, however peculiar this claim might seem, there is for Benjamin something messianic about the dead and the influence that they exert onto the living. Here, I do not mean messianic in the usual theological sense (although Benjamin is certainly a theologically based thinker) of bringing salvation from a higher place into the world. Instead, Benjamin's understanding of the corpse suggests a kind of salvation that is entirely immanent to the world, one that comes from the most humbled of objects, the human corpse itself. What it saves us from, you could say, is mythic violence itself including its own false promises of salvation. To the extent that the corpse emits an 'authority' of its own for Benjamin, that force works to trouble and subvert legal authority (among other forms) (Benjamin, 2006, p. 151). By keeping life and death connected and existing on a continuum with one another, Benjamin insures that the radical rejection of mythic violence that the dead body produces remains available to and important for the living as well. He shows that the living have a great deal to learn from the dead.[3]

FOUCAULT: LETTING DIE

In his own work on the question of death and its relationship to law and politics, Foucault focusses less on corpses per se and more on the kinds of regimes and institutions that emerge over the course of history which help to determine a particular relationship with death at any given time. In his lecture series 'Society Must be Defended', Foucault describes the rise of a biopolitical order in the late eighteenth century out of a previous order based on sovereignty. He tells us that the difference between these two epistemological regimes can be summarised in the following way:

> [The right of sovereignty] is the power to 'make' live and 'let' die .... And then this new [biopolitical] right is established: the right to make live and to let die. (Foucault, 1997, p. 241)

Considering the difference between these two regimes, Foucault (1997) tells us that under conditions of sovereignty

> in terms of his relationship with the sovereign, the subject is neither dead nor alive. From the point of view of life and death, the subject is neutral and it is thanks to the sovereign that the subject has the right to be alive, or possibly, the right to be dead. (p. 240)

Under conditions of biopolitics, Foucault tells us that the meaning of life and death profoundly changes. The function of power became entirely invested in managing populations, taxonomising and controlling all aspects of life. 'Making live' means that life itself became the key focus of governmentality. This means that death changes too. Foucault (1997) tells us that by the eighteenth century or so

> Death was no longer something that suddenly swooped down on life – as in an epidemic [or, one could also say, the whims of the sovereign]. Death was now something permanent, something that slips into life, permanently gnaws at it, diminishes it and weakens it. (p. 244)

In a sense, we can see that the term 'let die' is a bit misleading in this sense because biopolitics cannot really 'allow' death. Death can at best be postponed even for the regime's favoured groups. In this way, death becomes a problem for the various mechanisms of control (including legal ones) under conditions of biopolitics.

Accordingly, Foucault (1997) writes that:

> It is only natural that death [under conditions of biopolitics] should now be privatized, and should become the most private thing of all. In the right of sovereignty, death was the moment of the most obvious and most spectacular manifestation of the absolute power of the sovereign; death now becomes, in contrast, the moment when the individual escapes all power, falls back on himself and retreats, so to speak into his own privacy. Power no longer recognizes death. Power literally ignores death (p. 248).

This transformation of death from a political to a private affair has ramifications for the law as well. Under the sovereign regime, he tells us that with death

> we went from one court of law to another, from a civil or public life over life and death to a right to either eternal life or eternal damnation. Death also meant the transmission of the power of the dying, and that power was transmitted to those who survived him: last words, last recommendations, last wills and testaments, and so on. All of these powers are ritualized. (Foucault, 1997, pp. 247–248)

Because sovereignty is not eliminated but only brought under the logics of biopolitics, the legal order that arose with sovereignty remains in place. The concern with transmission of property, of last wills and the like all remain intact, more or less, in the new biopolitical regime. This legal regime must however coexist with a new sense of death and the challenges it poses to the legal persons that have now found themselves ensconced in a new biopolitical context.

IN RE WIDENING OF BEEKMAN STREET

Reading Benjamin and Foucault in tandem help to give us some perspective on the way that the law grapples with the legal status of the dead. Foucault's analysis suggests that sometime by the early nineteenth century, the law had to contend with the transformations that were occurring in the nature and status of death. If death becomes private then how does the law reflect that alteration? And if the dead body, as Benjamin tells us, lies somewhere between subject and object, to what extent can it be said to have rights of its own? How, in other words, does death haunt, interrupt and complicate legal personhood and with what implications for the living?

The case that I have chosen to focus on, *In re Widening of Beekman Street* (4 Bradf. (N.Y.) 503), initially came before the New York State Supreme Court in 1854 (it was decided in 1856). The case involved a strip of land that belonged to the Brick Presbyterian Church that had served as a burial ground. The city needed the land to expand Beekman Street, a major thoroughfare. The city had offered $28,000 to pay for the cost of relocating the dead bodies and burying them elsewhere. The church claimed that it was owed the money since the bodies were buried on its land. The families of the buried people, and in particular Maria Smith, whose father Moses Sherwood was buried on that stretch of land with a headstone, claimed that the money was due to them instead. The court ultimately ruled in favour of the heirs, ruling that some of the money had to compensate these families for the cost of reburial.

The vast majority of the case is a separate report filed in 1856 by Samuel B. Ruggles, a well-known lawyer and politician, as well as a large landholder. The court went along with his recommendations. The subtitle of this report, 'Report by Samuel B. Ruggles On the Claims of the City Corporation, The Vault-owners, the Occupants of Graves, and the Brick Presbyterian Church', already tells us something about the complexity of this case insofar as the 'Occupants of the Graves' are listed among the interested parties in this matter. Here, we already see something that will infuse all of Ruggles' report insofar as the nature of this particular constituency remains ever elusive. Are the 'Occupants of the Graves' merely bones and ashes – therefore purely objects – or are they in fact subjects who have perhaps the greatest interest of all in this matter insofar as it is their repose, their own graves, that are at issue?

A large part of Ruggles report is devoted to a survey of English common and canonical law. From the perspective of Foucault, this can be read as an attempt both to ground US law in an ancient tradition and, at the exact same time, to demonstrate a clear distinction from that practice, reflecting a newly privatised and, dare I say, more agentic concept of the corpse. Ruggles' historical survey engages especially with the question of whether the dead – as well as the sites of their burial – fall under the power of ecclesiastical or secular juridical authority.

Ruggles states that:

> In resorting to England for light on this subject, we encounter a body of law grown up under circumstances differing widely from our own. The jurisprudence of that country is peculiarly compounded, embracing largely the ecclesiastical element, from which ours is exempt; and it has given birth to anomalies which we are hardly required to adopt. This is strikingly manifest in the matter of the dead in which the partition of juridical authority between the Church and the State, forming one composite system, has materially narrowed the powers and the actions of the courts of common law. (*In Re Beekman*, p. 1117)

Here, we can see Ruggles attempting to make a distinction between English common law – which he held that we must respect since it is the basis for the authority of US law, as well as the basis (as I will show further) for his own decision – and English ecclesiastical law, which he tends to see as a usurper.

Ruggles notes, for example, that burial was originally a secular activity in England and only began to become viewed as an ecclesiastical matter, including burials in churchyards, in the eighth century (*In Re Beekman*, p. 1117). He further notes that after the Norman conquest 'the exclusive power of the ecclesiastics denominated, in legal phrase, "ecclesiastical cognizance", [and] became not only executive but judicial [in terms of its authority and power over the dead]' (*In Re Beekman,* p. 1118).

Ruggles strongly opposes this doctrine of ecclesiastical cognizance (the Brick Presbyterian Church advances this argument as the basis for its claim that it should be the party to be recompensed and not the families of those buried in its cemetery). Ruggles goes on to note that under this doctrine, when it comes to matters of any kind of violation of graves or any other disturbance, 'the heir could maintain no civil action for indecently, or even impiously, disturbing the remains of his buried ancestor, declaring the only remedy to belong to the parson' (*In Re Beekman*, p. 1118). Even the great English jurisprude, Edward Coke said, in a phrase that Ruggles deeply objects to, that 'the burial of the cadaver, that is, caro data vermibus [flesh given to worms] is nullius in bonis [belonging to no person] and belongs to ecclesiastical cognizance' (an argument that might anticipate Foucault's claim by the late eighteenth century, death becomes increasingly privatised)[4] (*In Re Beekman,* p. 1118).

Ruggles starts to make his case against ecclesiastical cognisance by carefully parsing Coke's understanding to argue that what is 'nullius in bonis' is not the corpse itself but only the burial so that 'the temporal office of burial had been brought within the exclusive legal cognizance of the Church' leaving the body with a separate legal status (*In Re Beekman*, p. 1119).

Ruggles goes on to say:

> the power thus exercised by the ecclesiastical tribunals was not spiritual in its nature, but merely temporal and juridical. It was a legal, secular authority, which they had gradually abstracted from the ancient civil courts, to which it had originally belonged; and that authority, from the very necessity of the case, in the State of New York, must now be vested in its secular courts of justice (*In Re Beekman*, p. 1118).

Ruggles further weakens the ecclesiastical position by noting, after doing a survey of Roman, Saxon and Gothic practices visá-vis the dead body, that 'the individual right was not extinguished [by the ecclesiastical takeover of burial after the Norman Conquest]; it was only absorbed by the church' (*In Re Beekman*, p. 1121). By recourse to ancient customs that predate the English church, Ruggles is claiming an individual right for the dead body that both pre- and postdates the ecclesiastical takeover of burial. In this way, he is both establishing an ancient and traditional basis for law even as he updates and modernizes that tradition to meet the needs of a new century and its biopolitical order.

Here, we come to central point I wish to make about this case: by prying the dead body away from ecclesiastical authority, Ruggles has freed the corpse from the clutches of the church but he has created a new problem insofar as the idea that it is the heirs who now 'own' the corpse comes into conflict with the corpse's own legal personhood (a concept which is itself necessary for allowing Ruggles to get that body out from the clutches of the church in the first place).[5] The entire question of the interruption of legal personhood becomes clearer when we examine the consequences of having made the corpse both independent (of the church) and newly dependent (upon the heir) at the same time.

Ruggles tells us, for example, that:

> the skeleton of the 'posthumous man' [he is referring here to Moses Sherwood] is now legally 'standing in court,' distinctly individualized – with his daughter [Maria Smith], next and nearest of kin, at his side, to ask, that the tribunal whose order for widening the street ejected him from the grave, will also direct his decent reinterment. (*In Re Beekman*, pp. 1121–1122)

Although he is, of course, not speaking in literal terms, by evoking the long dead Moses Sherwood as if he was actually standing next to his living daughter, Ruggles brings the personhood of the dead body right into the heart of the law, allowing a kind of legal haunting of the court by the subject that is most in question, even as it is also must emphatically not present, not 'standing' in that more literal sense.

The question this evocation (or haunting) raises, is how do the dead stand vis-á-vis the living? Can they be 'owned' by their heirs even as they evince a kind of agency, a legal presence and effect of their own?

Ruggles hesitates on this question, sometimes offering a robust protection of the corpses' own legal personhood and other times not. We see this tension, for example, in Ruggles' reflection on the judgement of Sir William Scott who gave a legal opinion in 1820 on whether a family could bury one of its members in an iron coffin. Because the church in question (like many churches in England and Europe) would rotate burials so that many people were buried in the same plot over a period of time, it was felt that an iron coffin would not disintegrate in the normal amount of time and thus prolong the period this person would spend in the gravesite. Ruggles quotes Scott as opining that:

> no mode of burial could be permitted which would prolong the natural decay of the body, or needlessly preserve its identity – that the lapse of a single generation is practically sufficient for mingling human remains with the earth, and destroying their identity – that the dead having no legal right to crowd the living, each buried generation must give way to its successors and that, therefore an iron coffin, which would unduly and unlawfully prolong the period for identifying the remains was ecclesiastically inadmissible – unless an extra fee were paid to the church. (*In Re Beekman*, p. 1121)

Here, we see that the long dead must give way to the newly dead in regular rotation. This implies – and we see this elsewhere in Ruggles' report as well – that the longer one is dead the more one's legal personhood disappears to be replaced by the kind of indifference to the corpse that for Ruggles is summarised by Coke's concept of 'caro data vermibus'.

In challenging Scott's ruling as something that is 'hardly … acceptable to the American mind', Ruggles goes on to write that

> The right to the individuality of a grave, if it exists at all, evidently must continue so long as the remains of the occupant can be identified – and the means of identifying can only be secured and preserved by separate burial. (*In Re Beekman*, p. 1122)

Phrases like 'if it exists at all' which Ruggles repeats at several points (in this case he's talking about the right 'to the individuality of a grave' elsewhere he talks about 'the right to the repose of the grave'), speaks to Ruggles' hesitation. We see in the preceding passage that Ruggles insists on the preservation of various rights for the dead person so long as they remain 'identifiable'. He argues that to mix other remains with a legally recognised person's remains is tantamount to 'destroy[ing] their individuality', violating, it seems the corpses' own legal rights (*In Re Beekman*, p. 1123). Over time, as the corpse decays into dirt and as memories of that person fade, it well eventually come to pass that the dead body has no material presence at all – at least not one that can be identified as such – in which case (and only in such a case) it appears that Ruggles would allow for interning someone else in that space or else using that space for entirely different purpose. Here, unlike as with Benjamin, for which there is never really a cutoff between the dead and the living, Ruggles seeks to establish a rough rule of thumb for how long a dead body remains connected, even tangentially to a living (and legal) personhood.

The other way that Ruggles thinks about the dead body (once again in keeping with Foucault's understanding of biopolitics) is as a piece of property that belongs, not to itself but to the heirs of that person. But this is not any ordinary piece of property. Ruggles tells us that

> the real question is not the disposable, marketable value of a corpse or its remains, as an article of traffic, but it is of the sacred and inherent right to its custody, in order decently to bury it, and secure its undisturbed repose'. (*In Re Beekman*, p. 1123)

There is no way to read this document, written virtually on the eve of the Civil War, without connecting this question of ownership of dead bodies with the question of ownership of the bodies of black slaves. As with slaves during this period, the dead body sits somewhere between a fully autonomous legal subject with rights, beginning above all with the right of self-ownership, and a piece of property that is effectively owned and controlled by others.[6] The main difference (one that favours the dead, at least the white dead) is that the rights of the corpse are considerably stronger and better protected than that of the slave. In the case of the corpse, the self-ownership of the living legal subject becomes transferred upon their death to another person. But even that other person – their heir – cannot dispose of this 'property' as they see fit.

CASES AFTER *IN RE WIDENING OF BEEKMAN STREET*

Ruggles' report and the case *In Re Widening of Beekman Street* more generally have become an oft cited and highly important aspect of US law when it comes to the treatment of dead bodies. In many of the court rulings that follow and cite *In Re Widening of Beekman Street*, there is a similar hesitation about the precise nature of the dead body. The same questions arise: is this a legal subject or a legal object? What rights, if any, does the corpse have? And, is this dead body property of any kind?

One key and telling subsequent case which heavily references *In Re Widening of Beekman Street* is an 1872 Rhode Island Supreme court case entitled *Pierce* v. *Proprietors of Swan Point Cemetery* 10 R.I. 227 (R.I. 1872). This case involved the child and the widow of a deceased man arguing over whether his widow could legitimately disinter and rebury his body somewhere else without his daughter's permission (something that had already taken place). The court ruled in the daughter's favour, arguing that the body had to be reburied where it had originally been located. In ruling in this way, the court found:

That there is no right of property in a dead body, using the word in its ordinary sense, may well be admitted. Yet the burial of the dead is a subject which interests the feelings of mankind to a much greater degree than many matters of actual property. There is a duty imposed by the universal feelings of mankind to be discharged by some one towards the dead; a duty, and we may also say a right, to protect from violation; and a duty on the part of others to abstain from violation. It may therefore be considered as a sort of *quasi*-property. (*Pierce* v. *Proprietors of Swan Point Cemetery*, p. 1125)

This case addresses the complexity of the dead person's identity even more plainly than *In Re Widening of Beekman Street*. The justices' hedge, the notion of the corpse as a 'quasi-property', gives the dead body a very strange and liminal legal existence. The judgement goes on to state:

Although, as we have said, the body is not property in the usually recognized sense of the word, we may consider it as a sort of *quasi*-property, to which certain persons may have rights, as they have duties to perform arising out of our common humanity. But the person having charge of it cannot be considered as the owner of it in any sense whatever. He holds it only as a sacred trust for the benefit of all who may, from family or friendship, have an interest in it. (*Pierce* v. *Proprietors of Swan Point Cemetery*, p. 1127)

But even this decision is not firm because the judgment also states:

Strictly speaking, according to the strict rules of the old common law, a dead man cannot be said to have rights. Yet it is common so to speak [and the justices go on to furnish many examples of legal cases doing just that] and the very fact of the common use of such language, and of its being used in such cases as we have quoted, justifies us in speaking of it as a right in a certain qualified sense and a right which ought to be protected. (*Pierce* v. *Proprietors of Swan Point Cemetery*, p. 1126)[7]

Here, we have a statement that the dead body is *not* a piece of property and furthermore an acknowledgement that the dead have no rights. And yet, it appears that the dead body nevertheless *is* a piece of property and *does* have rights. Part of this can be explained as a matter of perspective. When it looks from the perspective of the corpse, the law sees rights. When it looks from the perspective of the heirs, it sees property. Both views are correct producing an unresolvable legal doubleness.

The linguistic hesitations that we see here ('although', 'strictly speaking'), roughly mirror Ruggles' tendency to assert a right and then partially retract it by saying 'if it exists at all …'. These kinds of verbal tics help to demonstrate the way that when it comes to dead bodies, the law does not know what to say. As Benjamin might predict, in both of these cases, a resort to mysticism seems to be the only out (even if it is a *quasi*-property, it must be handled with due dignity. Christian civilisation demands certain proprieties, etc.). Here, the law reaches back to its own uncertain and obscured roots in order to reaffirm itself in the face of the aporia that death exposes in the heart of the law.[8]

THE CORPSE AS SYMBOL: AN 'UNSURPASSEDLY SPECTACULAR GESTURE'

In a somewhat later case, a 1905 judgement by the Supreme Court of Wisconsin, *Koerber* v. *Patek* 123 Wis. 453 (Wis. 1905), the justices stated:

> The duty of surviving spouse, parent, or child to provide proper burial for the corpse springs from the relationship to the person deceased. The desire to perform such service is founded in that respect and affection entertained for the relative, of whom the body, it is true, is but the symbol, but, for the few hours after life ceases, seems so to still represent him who was, that acts of care and protection to it are still paid to such departed. (p. 468)

Here, we see both the resort to mystification seen in previous cases as well as an invocation of the body as being a symbol. We see also the notion that over time that symbol becomes less connected to what it symbolises.

Although reducing the body to a symbol may seem to relegate it to a peripheral existence, Benjamin alerts us to the way that symbols are in fact deeply powerful modes of perception. The symbol for him carries a great danger because it is redolent of the kinds of idolatrous forms of language that come with mythic violence more generally. But the symbol as such has its uses nonetheless for Benjamin. It is precisely because the symbol lies at the heart of phantasm that it is such a critical source of resistance; like a corpse it can readily be reappropriated to do maximal damage to what it is meant to otherwise symbolise.

In his analysis of the German Baroque mourning plays in *Origin of German Tragic Drama,* Benjamin gives an example of how this might work. He talks about how the figure of Jesus was portrayed in these plays, not as perfectly transcendent, but rather very much as a human being with 'examples of birth, marriage, and funeral poems, of eulogies and victory congratulations, songs on the birth and death of Christ' (Benjamin, 1998, p. 183). Benjamin (1998) tells us further that in this way 'the symbolic becomes distorted into the allegorical' (p. 183). Finally, he tells us that '[i]t is an unsurpassably spectacular gesture to place even Christ in the realm of the provisional, the everyday, the unreliable' (Benjamin, 1998, p. 183).

Here, the ultimate symbol of transcendence, Jesus Christ himself, becomes a basis for radically undermining what he symbolises. This is an 'unsurpassably spectacular gesture' which uses ordinary life to demystify and expose symbolic authority. By the same token, we can see that the dead body achieves something similar in law. The dead body seems at first glance to be the acme of a passive object, meekly submitting to whatever the law says that it is. But as we have seen in practice, the law cannot quite decide what the dead body is, cannot determine if it is a subject or an object, and resorts to calls for reverence and respect which are outside of the scope of the law itself. This leaves the law vulnerable to exposure and demystification as well.

Although the justices in *Koerber* v. *Patek* saw the corpse as a symbol for the living person, we can just as easily say that the corpse can be read as a symbol for itself. To grapple with the reality of that body (as courts are forced to do), with its location, its basis, its characteristics, means (as with the Baroque portrayals of Jesus) to render this ultimately abstracted symbol of a legal person into something tangible. This too can be read as an 'unsurpassably spectacular gesture'. The spectacularity of this gesture takes aim at the spectacle itself. It fights fire with fire. Confronted with the reality of a dead body, the symbol – which is something that the law is generally very comfortable with and sees as no threat at all – becomes a way for that body to subvert the inner sanctums of law.

This should not be overread as meaning that the law somehow collapses in the face of a dead body. Instead, the law is discovering its own limits. The truth is that the law has no power over a dead body. It can, of course, make rulings about what to do with it, where to dispose of it, who should pay for burial and reburial, etc. It has that kind of power but at the same time it is revealed that the law has no true control over the kind of legal person that the dead body becomes. This person has escaped from the clutches of the law (it has been 'let [to] die') and it is the lingering effects of that person's presence that exposes the law's own emptiness.

The corpse's escape from the law suggests a much more critical point as well. Insofar as the corpse is connected to the living human body (not just by Benjamin but by the courts themselves), the failure of the law to determine the dead person suggests that it might not be able to control the living person either, something that presents a much greater threat to the law's jurisdiction and power.

It would be far easier if the law could just take the position of Diogenes (who is actually cited in *In re Widening of Beekman Street* as the epitome of what *not* to do) and say that once we are dead, it does not matter what happens to our dead bodies. Let them be worm food as Coke suggested! But in fact the law retreats from this position. Even Coke insisted that some kind of legal authority – in this case ecclesiastical law – be in charge of the corpse. The law will not fully abandon personhood for the dead body because it threatens abandoning personhood in general. The dead body is not enough of an unperson for the law to confidently write off. Any loss of control over those that the law has 'let die' suggests a loss of control over those that it 'make[s] live' too.

This is why I suggested earlier that the dead body threatens in some sense not just the taxonomies that the law would like to impose but in some sense the law itself. Again this does not mean that the law is literally threatened by its encounter with the dead but it does suggest that the law's own nothingness is exposed when it meets an object whose own lingering somethingness exposes the emptiness of the law by contrast.

CONCLUSION

If the dead body successfully interrupts the legal person (if I have been persuasive) what is the product of that interruption? What kind of person emerges beyond the confines of legal personhood? If we think of legal persons as reflecting the law's anxiety about its status, even its existence, then it seems that legal personhood must share these same features, namely the fact that a legal person is different from an actual person. The fact that it takes a dead body to help us figure that out shows how much legal personhood has de facto become or stood in for our actual personhood, whatever that might be.

What kind of personhood is suggested by the dead body? On the surface of things, this seems like a singularly bad direction for inquiry insofar as a dead body doesn't do anything, doesn't seem to promise much in terms of serving as a model for what other kinds of persons we can be as living beings. Yet, as I've been arguing, there is one way that the dead person *does* serve as a good model for us. This is in terms of the way that the dead body counter-projects all of the myths and phantasms of law, among other things. The dead body can teach us, the living, how to do the same thing, showing that we are not doomed to reflect the projections that purportedly constitute us (but do not). In this way, I think that it is important that, rather than constantly telling ourselves what the dead mean and are (as we saw the justices in the cases I discussed doing) we allow instead the dead to tell us what we are not. That is to say, if we allow ourselves to stand in the path of the counter-projection from the dead, we may well experience the kinds of disruptions that I have been looking at in this chapter to disrupt our sense of legal personhood as well.

I think what emerges from this disrupted kind of personhood is neither 'true' and authentically us, nor is it entirely innocent of law, insofar as law has long been involved in forming and shaping the living. Rather than exposing the true self under the legal person, I think what we find is a hodge-podge of identities that overlap. Some are related to law and some are not. I don't think we should try to find a terrain that is entirely free of law because that strikes me as just an invitation to further phantasm and projection.

The legal cases that I looked at only offer us the dimmest sense of these kinds of outcomes or possibilities. The law is always magisterial; it never says 'I don't know what to say'. It's poise of control is meant to be convincing. Even so, just as in *the Matrix* when a slight glitch in the field of vision hinted at vast problems behind the scenes, the cracks that I have looked at in legal discourse point to possible deeper disturbances in the field of law. It also points to other possibilities, ways of being that the law can't and won't admit even to as it can't help raising them as it confronts the facticity and materiality of the dead.

The key point to keep in mind is that the dead body is never as distant from living human beings as the law might want you to think. As previously noted, what's true for the dead body is also true for those of us who are alive and so the cracks in the edifice of law that are revealed in the cases that I have treated above are evidence of cracks in the edifice of our living personhood too. If we allow ourselves to be interrupted and disrupted while alive, it is important to note that we aren't starting over, coming up with an entirely new identity in doing so. We have all the history, all the sedimentation, all the memories and canons of our life as part of the scene that we face. With this basis, our interrupted legal personhood can be the source of radically new ways of being and thinking, possibilities that can be spotted, at least by negative implication, even from the most ordinary of legal discourses. In a time like the current moment of the pandemic, perhaps the notion that the dead can be critical co-conspirators rather than simply persons who are now lost to us may be, not only a matter of comfort, but also of renewed determination and mutual support as we face unprecedented challenges both legal and otherwise.

NOTES

1. Derrida's conception of haunting and 'hauntology' comes to mind here. In this case too the haunting in question is less supernatural and more a result of the lingering effects of material aspects that can't be accounted for in the law's own self-understanding. See Derrida, 1994.

2. For more on the way that burial helps to hide the corpse and restore the image of the person that was when they were alive see Laqueur (2015). See also Harrison (2005).

3. The opposite is true as well. In 'On the Concept of History' Benjamin (2003) tells us '*even the dead* will not be safe from the enemy if he is victorious. And this enemy has never ceased to be victorious' (p. 391).

4. English law itself has evolved its own position on the question of dead bodies as property. A key nineteenth century legal case on this issues was Williams v. Williams (1882) when a man, trying to circumvent an English law against cremation, in a codicil to his will 'gave' his corpse to a Ms Williams in order to have her burn it. When his wishes were not followed by his executors (he was buried), Ms Williams had the body disinterred and sent to Milan for cremation. She sued the executors of his will for the cost of cremation. The court ruled against her saying that dead bodies cannot be property and therefore no one can legally will it to someone else. See Williams v. Williams (1882). Much more recently, in *Anstey* v. *Mundle* (2016), a man originally from Jamaica expressed a wish to be buried there next to his mother. The court ruled that a will could in fact influence the fate of a (now) dead body. See Anstey v. Mundle (2016). Here too, then, the question of the nature and 'ownership' of the corpse is a shifting and complicated issue. For a good account of the development of the legal regime in England as pertains to dead bodies and also to the relationship between those bodies and (other) material objects – including the complicated legal concept of the deodand and its subsequent elimination – see Trabsky (2019).

5. Ruggles gives a sense of his passionate objection to ecclesiastical cognisance when he writes 'if no one has any legal interest in a corpse, no one can legally determine the place of its internment, nor exclusively retain its custody. A son will have no legal right to retain the remains of his father, nor a husband of his wife, one moment after death .... The dead, deprived of the legal guardianship, however partial which the Church so long had thrown around them, and left unprotected by the civil courts, will become, in law, nothing but public nuisances and their custody will belong only to the guardians of the public health, to remove and destroy the offending matter with all practicable economy and dispatch' (*In Re Beekman*, p. 1119).

6. This confusion can traced at least in part to John Locke, who also muddled boundaries between subjects based on hierarchical relations (notably men and women, masters and servants and parents and children). See Locke (1988). See also Patterson (2018). When this chapter was presented as a paper, Val Napoleon pointed out a similar blurring of boundaries is applied to the question of indigenous bones in the USA and other settler colonial spaces, bones that continue to be held by anthropologists and other collectors.

7. The judgement goes on to cite a panel on the codification of laws in Massachusetts as stating that the common law 'is not in its nature and character an absolutely fixed, inflexible system, like the statute law' (Pierce v. Proprietors of Swan Point Cemetery, p.1126).

8. A similar stance can be seen in other cases as well such as Renihan v. Wright or Enos v. Snyder.

REFERENCES

Books and Articles

Benjamin, W. (1996). Critique of violence. In M. Bullock & M. W. Jennings (Eds.), *Walter Benjamin: Selected writings Volume I, 1913–1926*. Cambridge, MA: Harvard University Press.

Benjamin, W. (1998). *Origin of German tragic drama*. New York, NY: Verso.

Benjamin, W. (2003). On the concept of history. In H. Eiland & M. W. Jennings (Eds.), *Walter Benjamin: Selected Writings Volume 4, 1938–1940*. Cambridge, MA: Harvard University Press (Belknap).

Benjamin, W. (2006). The storyteller. In H. Eiland & M. W. Jennings (Eds.), *Walter Benjamin: Selected writings Volume 3, 1935–1938* (pp. 143–166). Cambridge, MA: Harvard University Press.

Derrida, J. (1994). *Specters of Marx: The state of the debt, the work of mourning and the new international*. New York, NY: Routledge.

Foucault, M. (1997). *Society must be defended: Lectures at the Collège de France 1975–1976*. New York, NY: Picador.

Harrison, R. P. (2005). *The dominion of the dead.* Chicago, IL: University of Chicago Press.
Laqueur, T. W. (2015). *The work of the dead.* Princeton, NJ: Princeton University Press.
Locke, J. (1988). In P. Laslett (Ed.), *Two treatises of government* (Chapter V., pp. 288–289). Cambridge: Cambridge University Press.
Martel, J. (2018). *Unburied bodies: Subversive corpses and the authority of the dead.* Amherst, MA: Amherst College Press.
Patterson, O. (2018). *Slavery and social death.* Cambridge, MA: Harvard University Press.
Trabsky, M. (2019). *Law and the dead: Technology, relations and institutions.* New York, NY: Routledge.

Legal Cases

US Law

Enos v. *Snyder* 181 Cal. 68 (63 Pac. 170).
In Re Widening of Beekman Street, 4 Bradf (N.Y.) 503, *The American ruling cases as determined by the courts; Including the fundamental cases of England and Canada; also all reviewing and illustrating cases of material value from the latest official report, completely annotated Volume II.* Chicago: National Law Book Co., 1912–1920.
Koerber v. *Patek*, 123 Wis. 453 (Wis. 1905).
Renihan v. *Wright*, 125 Ind. 536.
William G. Pierce and Wife v. *Proprietors of Swan Point Cemetery and Almira T. Metcalf*, 10 R.I. 227 (Rhode Island Supreme Court, March Term 1872) in *The American ruling cases as determined by the courts; Including the fundamental cases of England and Canada; also all reviewing and illustrating cases of material value from the latest official report, completely annotated Volume II.* Chicago: National Law Book Co., 1912–1920.

English Law

Anstey v. *Mundle* [2016] EWHC 1073 (Ch).
Williams v. *Williams* [1882] 20 ChD 659.